MW00463088

31 WOMEN OF THE BIBLE

WHO THEY WERE AND WHAT WE CAN LEARN FROM THEM TODAY

TABLE OF CONTENTS

INTRODUCTION

"It begins with a character, usually, and once he stands up on his feet and begins to move, all I can do is trot along behind him with a paper and pencil trying to keep up long enough to put down what he says and does."
— William Faulkner

Faulkner's words about writing fiction are also true for reading divine truth.

For all its emphasis on religious places and holy ideas, the Bible, in the final analysis, is about characters. "It begins with a character"—the triune God. It then proceeds to tell one great story made up of countless smaller stories. At the heart of all this action, on every page of Scripture, we meet fascinating, real-life people. These are characters worth our time and attention.

31 Women of the Bible has been written to remind readers of Scripture of three great truths:

1. *Women have played an indispensable role in the great story of God.* Though the Bible is without question dominated by towering male figures like Abraham, Moses, David, Pilate, and Paul, it's far from a sexist book (as some have charged). From Sarah to Mary and from Esther to Elizabeth, a number of the most important heroes of the Christian faith were female.

2. *Bible people were flawed, flesh-and-blood folks—not unlike us.* We have a tendency to

idealize Scriptural saints; however, it's not necessary to either romanticize or idolize them to appreciate them. (It's also not healthy!)

3. *The most vivid and valuable lessons come not from a lecture but from a life.*

In the pages that follow, you'll find:

- A concise summary of each woman's appearance in Scripture, viewed through the lens of our modern culture

- Surprising revelations that may cause you to rethink what you thought you knew about each woman

- Bible passages, ripe for memorization, that capture the essence of each woman's experience

- Helpful prompts for applying the principles of each woman's story to your own life

- Thought-provoking questions to help you find common ground with the heroes of the Christian faith

Our hope is that as you "trot along behind" the thirty-one women featured in these pages, noting what each "says and does," you'll be able to "keep up long enough" to be challenged, encouraged, warned, and helped.

"A woman who fears the LORD will be praised."
— Proverbs 31:30

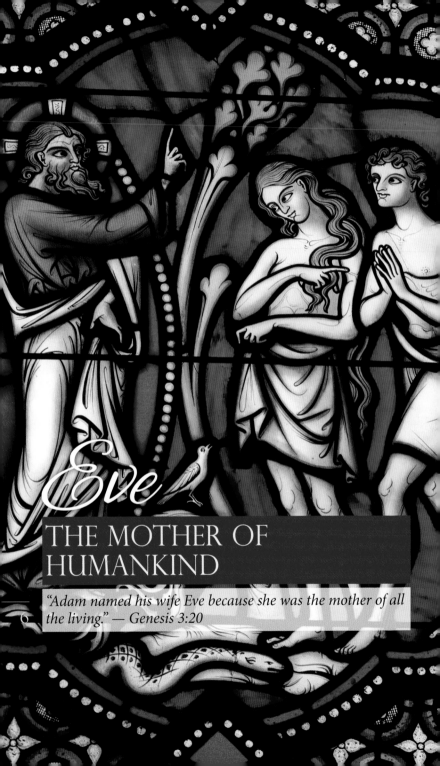

Eve
THE MOTHER OF HUMANKIND

"Adam named his wife Eve because she was the mother of all the living." — Genesis 3:20

6

E ve enjoys the distinction of being the first woman—*in all of human history*. Talk about special.

When God decided to make human creatures "in His own image" (Gen 1:27), he created the male first (see Gen 2:7). A few verses later we read, "Then the LORD God said, 'It is not good for the man to be alone. I will make a helper as his complement'" (Gen 2:18).

Some regard this statement as demeaning—to Eve in particular, and all women in general. Nothing could be further from the truth. In calling Eve Adam's "helper," God used a word that's employed elsewhere in the Old Testament to speak of God himself as the uplifting helper of his people (Deut 33:7, 26; Pss 33:20; 70:5; 115:9, 10, 11; 146:5). Eve was God's very tangible way of saying, "Adam, you need help!"

And such help! The verb *make* means "to fashion." In other words, Adam's new "helper" would be a work of art by the ultimate Creator. It gets even better. The word *complement* means "suitable or corresponding to." The idea is that Eve would fit Adam like a jigsaw puzzle piece. She would supply strengths he lacked, and vice versa. Ultimately, Eve would be the "very good" solution (Gen 1:31) to Adam's "not good" solitary existence.

And so it was. God crafted this exquisite creature to help and to complement Adam. As the first human female companion and wife, Eve experienced wonders in life none of us can fathom: glorious face-to-face walks and talks with God, marriage as it was meant to be, creation in all its piercing beauty and none of its brokenness.

How long did this perfect bliss last? A few weeks? Only a weekend? However long it was, Eve had it. She tasted it. Then, inexplicably, she gave in to the desire to taste something more. Therein lies the great liar's great lie: even perfection is not enough.

Genesis 3 tells the tragic and mysterious story of how Eve was approached, tempted, and ultimately deceived by the serpent (or Satan, see 2 Cor 11:3). He somehow aroused within her a nagging doubt about God's good heart. Or else he manipulated Eve's identity as one who *resembled* God into a desire to *replace* God. However he did it, the evil one convinced Eve to defy her Creator. But before we put a disproportionate amount of blame on Eve's shoulders, the Bible makes it clear that her husband, Adam, "was with her" (Gen 3:6). For incomprehensible reasons, he stood by passively, saying and doing nothing as his wife debated with the devil. She had barely swallowed the forbidden fruit before he was chewing it too.

Talk about tragic. The result was exactly what God had warned—death. The immediate death of innocence, intimacy, and peace. The catastrophic end to a harmonious relationship with God, with others, with creation itself. Gone were virtues like vulnerability, trust, and selflessness. Expulsion from Eden followed, meaning a loss of access to God and to the tree of life. Adam and Eve could only look back over their shoulders at paradise and wonder what might have been.

Post-Eden, they did their best to carve out a new life. Eve became a mom to three sons: Cain, Abel, and Seth (and surely to daughters as well). At some point she faced the parental nightmare of having to bury her secondborn. Making this tragic situation worse was the fact that Abel's death came at the hands of his big brother.

How or when or where Eve died, God alone knows. How tragic that this special woman, "the mother of all the living," also played a prominent role in bringing death into the world.

In a sense, Eve's life prefigures every life. Each one will be special. Beautiful. Marked by doubt and disobedience. Marred by the tragedy of sin and utterly dependent on the One who is able to reverse its curse.

THE TAKEAWAY

From Eve's beautiful and tragic experience, we glean a couple of truths.

One, life works best when we trust and obey the explicit Word of God. We have an enemy who uses deceit in order to destroy (see John 8:44; 1 Pet 5:8). Since we are continually subjected to a chorus of competing voices, we have to be careful. We can know the enemy is at work when we

find ourselves entertaining the notion that God's heart is suspect, that his way is restrictive, and that doing his will leads to a diminished life. The devil is crafty. He is able to speak even through well-intentioned people (see Mark 8:31–33). It's only because, in the words of Martin Luther, "the right man [is] on our side" that we are able to stand against his enticements.

Two, marriage works best when husbands and wives work in tandem—men using their masculine strength to be protective servant-leaders and women using their feminine strength to be supportive helpers. If you are married, ask God to show you specific ways to become a stronger ally to your spouse.

FOOD FOR THOUGHT

1. Overall, do you find yourself liking or disliking Eve? Why?

2. We've all experienced loss, but Eve lost *paradise*. What do you think that was like?

3. What does it say about God that he allowed Eve, the mother of sin, to become an ancestor of the One—Jesus—who eventually defeated sin?

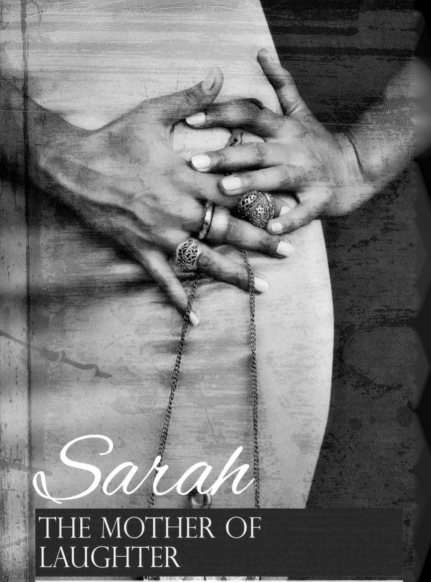

Sarah

THE MOTHER OF LAUGHTER

"But the Lord asked Abraham, 'Why did Sarah laugh, saying, "Can I really have a baby when I'm old?" Is anything impossible for the Lord? At the appointed time I will come back to you, and in about a year she will have a son.'

"Sarah denied it. 'I did not laugh,' she said, because she was afraid. But He replied, 'No, you did laugh.'"
— *Genesis 18:13–15*

The Bible doesn't reveal how Sarah (Sarai) reacted when she learned that Abram wanted her to be his wife (see Gen 11:29). We're also not told how she handled the fact that she was barren (see 11:30), though we could probably imagine how devastating this realization was.

We don't know Sarah's response the day her husband came home and told her they'd be moving south and west to Canaan (see Gen 12:1–5). Did she ask questions about his far-fetched story? *A supernatural call from a God named Yahweh? A wagonload of grandiose promises? An old childless couple producing a great nation? Worldwide fame? Blessed so much the blessing would spill out onto the entire world? Really, Abram?*

What does a sixty-five-year-old infertile woman do with all that? How confused and depressed must Sarah have felt? To her credit, if she thought her seventy-five-year-old hubby had been drinking or stricken with sudden dementia, she kept such thoughts to herself. She gathered up her belongings, and hand in hand they set out (see Gen 12:6–9).

How about Abram's boneheaded attempt in Egypt to pass her off as his sister (see Gen 12:10–20)? How did Sarah respond to that? Was she more wounded or angry? When he had to arm his servants and embark on a dangerous mission to rescue their nephew Lot, who had gotten caught up in a tribal war (see Gen 14:1–24), did Sarah worry, cry, panic, or pray?

There's so much we don't know: how Sarah felt each time her husband gave her another wild-eyed report of a strange, divine vision (see Gen 15:1–21); what she thought when Abram came home one day and told her Yahweh had abruptly changed their names to Abraham and Sarah (see Gen 17:5, 15).

Only in a couple of instances do we get a glimpse into Sarah's heart. One of these came after more than a decade of Abraham's "God-will-give-us-a-baby" talk. The long-suffering Sarah suggested a plan—maybe just to shut her husband up. "Since the LORD has prevented me from bearing children, go to my slave; perhaps through her I can build a family" (Gen 16:2). Abraham signed off on the idea. He slept with Hagar, and the result was a boy, Ishmael.

Immediately Sarah was the polar opposite of happy. Though the whole thing had been her own idea, just the sight of that gloating Hagar holding that cooing baby ripped her soul in two. Sarah lashed out at her husband. She turned bitter and mean (see Gen 16:5–16).

After another thirteen long years passed, we once again see the raw reaction of Sarah when three visitors showed up with shocking news (see Gen 18:1–15). Abraham asked her if she wouldn't mind whipping up a meal for their surprise company. She did so and then retreated to her tent. Only when she heard one of the visitors speak her name did she begin to listen in on their hushed conversation.

That's when the eighty-nine-year-old Sarah heard the speaker say that she would become a mother within the year. The thought was too crazy, too unthinkable, too outlandish. Sarah started to laugh and then caught herself.

To be fair, it was more a quiet chuckle than a loud guffaw. And it was driven more by amused disbelief than derisive scorn. Still, the Lord heard it. And, when he asked Abraham why Sarah would dare doubt the word of Almighty God, she got flustered and scared. She tried to deny her reaction. The Lord wasn't buying it.

At long last, when the child of the promise finally arrived a year later, Sarah's response was genuine, unapologetic laughter (see Gen 21:6). It was the unparalleled joy of a first-time mom, the unedited glee of someone who'd finally received a long-anticipated gift. In fact, when these two wrinkled, old, new parents discovered they couldn't stop smiling and giggling, they decided to just go ahead and name the boy *Isaac*, which means "laughter."

Maybe the old saying is true after all: "The person who laughs last, laughs best."

THE TAKEAWAY

If you are facing a grim situation, one option is to give in to bitterness and despair (not recommended). A better option is to reflect on the story of Sarah.

At the height of her hopelessness, Sarah was on the receiving end of perhaps the best rhetorical question in the Bible. As she struggled against doubt and cynicism, she was asked, "Is anything impossible for the LORD?" (Gen 18:14).

The answer is, of course, no. Nothing is impossible for God. Lots of things are difficult for us to endure, but nothing is too hard for God.

It's this one truth that can produce laughter even when nothing else can.

FOOD FOR THOUGHT

1. When's the last time you laughed until the tears rolled down your face?

2. What surprises you most about Sarah? What do you admire most about her?

3. What "impossible" situation are you currently facing?

Hagar

SEEING THE GOD WHO SEES

"So she called the LORD who spoke to her: The God Who Sees, for she said, 'In this place, have I actually seen the One who sees me?'" — Genesis 16:13

H agar was Egyptian by birth (see Gen 16:1). How she became a servant of the Mesopotamian Sarai (eventually known as Sarah, the wife of Abraham, the patriarch of the nation of Israel), no one can say for sure.

More than a decade after God's promise to make Abraham the father of a great nation, Sarah was still childless. Finally, in her mid-seventies, with equal parts frustration and desperation, Sarah "took Hagar, her Egyptian slave, and gave her to her husband Abram as a wife for him. . . . He slept with Hagar" (Gen 16:3–4).

This was a common occurrence in ancient Near Eastern culture. Men took concubines. Barren wives often *gave* concubines to their husbands if they saw that as the only way to provide their husbands with an heir (see also Gen 30:1–6).

Though Sarah's plan worked like a charm, the whole thing was ill-conceived. God wasn't looking for Sarah's help. Hers was a fleshly, desperate act of fear, not a God-honoring step of faith. And Abraham's complicity in her scheme is regrettable. Not surprisingly, these choices unleashed an avalanche of dysfunction in Abraham's household.

The pregnant Hagar gloated and acted contemptuously toward her mistress. This resulted in the bitter Sarah reaming out her husband. Abraham basically threw up his hands and said, "Whatever!" When Sarah made life miserable for her servant, Hagar decided enough was enough. She packed her belongings and hit the road.

She headed south and west and might have eventually made it all the way back to Egypt, except that the Angel of the Lord intercepted her. He gave Hagar this uncomfortable command: "Go back to your mistress and submit to her mistreatment" (Gen 16:9). But then he sweetened the deal with a staggering promise: "I will greatly multiply your offspring, and they will be too many to count" (16:10).

After learning she was carrying a son, being instructed to name him Ishmael (which means "God hears"), and receiving assurances that the Lord was watching over her, Hagar's entire mood changed. If she was not already a believer in Yahweh, she seems to have become one that day. She began referring to him as "The God Who Sees" (Gen 16:13).

She returned and had the baby. For more than thirteen years Ishmael was the little prince. He ruled the roost—until the day the almost-ninety-year-old Sarah turned up pregnant. Suddenly, all that unresolved domestic tension returned with a vengeance. When Sarah caught the teenaged

Ishmael mocking her precious little Isaac, she demanded that Abraham "drive out this slave with her son" (Gen 21:10).

As the doting father of both boys, Abraham was devastated by this ultimatum (see Gen 21:11). But then God told him, "Do not be concerned about the boy and your slave. Whatever Sarah says to you, listen to her, because your offspring will be traced through Isaac. But I will also make a nation of the slave's son because he is your offspring" (Gen 21:12–13).

It's unsettling to even ponder Hagar's experience the following day. In accordance with God's seemingly callous command, Abraham sent them off into the wilderness. Hagar and the boy walked until all their water—and all their hope—was gone. When Hagar collapsed, weeping in the dust, once again the angel of God met her in her desperation. He told her not to fear. He reiterated his promise to make Ishmael "a great nation" (Gen 21:18). Then, the God who sees and hears, the God who protects and provides, the God who shows up and comes through, revealed a desert well. Hagar and Ishmael were saved.

They settled in the Wilderness of Paran. When the time came, Hagar arranged for Ishmael to marry a nice girl "from the land of Egypt"—her home country (Gen 21:21). What she did after that is anyone's guess, though it's not a stretch to imagine that her final years included enjoying her twelve grandsons (see Gen 25:12–16) and an unspecified number of granddaughters.

THE TAKEAWAY

Many of the details of Hagar's story are disturbing: As a servant and concubine, she was treated like property. She suffered mistreatment to the point of having no other recourse but to run. And she was sent into the desert by the father of her child. You can't study Hagar's life without wincing.

But at least two of the anecdotes in Genesis are extremely encouraging. In Hagar's darkest and bleakest moments, God showed up. In the nick of time, he revealed himself and promised: *I know. I see. I hear. I care. You are safe. You have a future. You don't have to fear.*

Suffering isn't fun for anyone. That much is true. But here's another truth: any difficulty that leads us to the presence of God is more than worth it.

FOOD FOR THOUGHT

1. What do you learn about God's character in the ups and downs of Hagar's life?

2. What lessons could a person who is dealing with difficult family relationships glean from the story of Hagar?

3. Have you had experiences where God dramatically revealed himself to you in the middle of great trauma or trouble? What specifically happened?

Lot's Wife

A CAUTIONARY TALE ABOUT WORLDLINESS

"Remember Lot's wife!" — Luke 17:32

L ot's wife is one of the many unnamed characters of Scripture. We don't know her background or how or where she and Lot met. We only know she was a mother of two daughters (see Gen 19:15) and that she lived with Lot in the notoriously wicked city of Sodom.

Lot, for the record, was the nephew of the great Abraham. Originally from Ur (a Chaldean city near the Persian Gulf), Lot had moved west with his uncle and grandfather to Haran (see Gen 11:31–32). Later, when God told Abraham to journey south, promising to bless him and the world through him, Lot wisely tagged along.

They passed through Canaan. They spent time in Egypt. Pretty quickly the abundant material blessings God poured out on Abraham spilled over into Lot's life. Suddenly the land could not sustain the huge herds of both men. Lot chose to move farther east. He unwisely "set up his tent near Sodom"—despite the fact that the city of Sodom had a notorious reputation for evil (Gen 13:12–13).

When we next see Lot, he's conducting business at the Sodom city gate, and he's living in a house (not a tent) in (not near) the city (see Gen 19:1–5). Sodom had obviously become home for Lot.

It's possible this is when and where Lot met his wife. But even if she wasn't *from* Sodom, we do know she didn't want to *leave* there—not even when God announced judgment and warned Lot and his family to flee. Lot's wife was reluctant to go even when two angels compassionately took her by the hand and led her and her family out of the city. "Run for your lives! Don't look back and don't stop!" (Gen 19:17), an angel warned Lot and his family just before God unleashed his fury.

It was then, without actually saying *anything*, that Lot's wife revealed *everything* about her heart and her character, about her values and priorities. As divine judgment rained down, Lot's wife "looked back and became a pillar of salt" (Gen 19:26).

Late in his ministry, Jesus was talking with his disciples about his second coming. He told them the end times would be like "it was in the days of Noah" (Luke 17:26). You'll recall that even while Noah built a massive ark, he fervently warned his neighbors of a catastrophic judgment to come. People yawned and went on with their lives as usual.

And then, just in case his followers weren't fully grasping the gravity of his words, Jesus warned that in the last days (similar to "the days of Lot"; Luke 17:28), people will be so preoccupied with all the stuff of this world—"eating, drinking, buying, selling, plant-ing, building"—they will miss the signs. Or they will ignore them. Either way, they will not be prepared.

To illustrate his point, Jesus said those memorable words: "Remember Lot's wife!" (Luke 17:32). Remember the woman who married a successful man and probably enjoyed many of the finer things in life. Remember the woman who seemed to be oblivious to the evil around her. Remember the woman who resisted and ultimately spurned the compassionate mercy of God. Remember the woman who, when she was staring the eternal in the face, could think only of temporal things.

Lot's wife serves as a cautionary tale about the deadliness of worldliness. That she relished living in an evil culture like Sodom's was bad enough. That such a culture lived *in her* proved to be her undoing.

THE TAKEAWAY

It's easy to forget the danger of getting too chummy with a corrupt world. The process is almost imperceptible. It always happens by degrees. A concession here, a deci-sion there, and before we know it we're a long way from where we ever intended to be. Our hearts are set on all the wrong things. Our values are warped, and we are treasuring possessions that not only will not last but may actually destroy us.

This is why we need the pithy warning of Jesus to "re-member Lot's wife." We will never find the security we crave by fixing our hope on insecure things.

No one, of course, knows when Christ will return. But surely when that day comes, the things treasured most by our culture (financial wealth, physical beauty, fit bodies, designer clothing, elegant homes, career success, etc.) will be worthless.

Only a fool stares longingly at the temporal when facing the eternal.

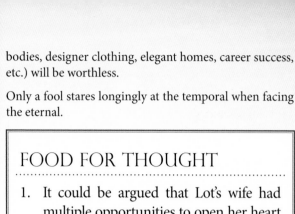

FOOD FOR THOUGHT

1. It could be argued that Lot's wife had multiple opportunities to open her heart to God and to eternal realities. After all, she was related (through marriage) to Abraham, the paragon of faith, and had an up-close-and-personal encounter with angelic beings. Why do you suppose she didn't? Why is it so difficult for people to see beyond the temporal stuff of this world?

2. An idol is anything other than God that we look to for life or meaning or rescue or security or happiness. What are the things that rival God in your own life?

3. If you look closely, you may discover some of the same "Lot's wife" tendencies in your own heart. What can you practically do to ensure that you keep your eyes and heart focused on God and not "look back" on things of this world?

Rebekah

PRACTICALLY PERFECT IN EVERY WAY

"Isaac loved Esau because he had a taste for wild game, but Rebekah loved Jacob." — *Genesis 25:28*

There's so much to admire about Rebekah.

She came from "good stock." A native of the city of Aram-naharaim in Mesopotamia (see Gen 24:10), she was the daughter of Bethuel and the sister of Laban. Her great-uncle was the legendary Hebrew patriarch Abraham.

She was a head turner. The Bible describes Rebekah not simply as attractive but as "very beautiful" (Gen 24:16; see also 26:7). When we meet her in Scripture, she's only a young maiden (she's called a "girl" five times in Genesis 24), but in that introduction we see that Rebekah was as good-looking on the inside as she was on the outside.

She was a servant. At the city well, when Rebekah encountered Abraham's servant (who had been sent by Abraham on a long journey to find a wife for his son Isaac), she not only gave him water to drink but also graciously offered to water all his camels.

She was kind and hospitable. After only a brief conversation, we witness Rebekah warmly inviting Abraham's servant to lodge at her home (see Gen 24:23–25).

She was courageous and adventurous. After Abraham's servant explained to her and her family how she was the very precise answer to his very specific prayer for a wife for Abraham's son Isaac, her father and brother could only say, "This is from the LORD" (Gen 24:50). After a night of lavish gift giving and celebrating, the servant was ready to pack up Rebekah and return to Canaan the very next morning. It was all so sudden, her mom and brother wanted a few more days with her. When they let her make the decision, she bravely replied, "I will go" (24:58). Just like that, she was off to begin a brand-new life.

She understood the struggle of childlessness. Despite a loving relationship (see Gen 24:67), Rebekah endured the bitter pain of infertility for the first *twenty* years of her marriage to Isaac. When Isaac interceded for her, she finally conceived (see 25:21, 26). It was a difficult pregnancy, and not until she inquired of the Lord did she learn why: she was carrying twins with very different destinies. The firstborn, a son, was covered with red hair. Isaac and Rebekah named him *Esau.* The younger twin, also a boy, came out of the womb with a firm grip on his older brother's heel. He was named *Jacob* (because the Hebrew noun *heel* and Hebrew phrase *to watch from behind* sound similar to *Jacob*). Unfortunately, Rebecca's actions as the mother of these nonidentical twins have caused many Bible readers to wince.

She had an unhealthy relationship with her son Jacob. Someone once described a boy as "a noise with dirt on it." That was Esau to a T. He was busy and active, rough and rugged. He grew up to become a "guy," a real "man's man." His love for hunting, combined with his father's taste for wild game, made for a special connection between the two. Anybody with a pulse could tell Esau was the apple of Isaac's eye.

Maybe this is why Rebekah gravitated toward Jacob. He was quieter, a thinker and dreamer, always coming up with some new scheme. While Isaac and Esau had bonded over the great outdoors, Jacob and Rebekah connected indoors. He was, in our vernacular, a "homebody," a true "mama's boy."

All this parental favoritism reached a toxic level when the aged, blind Isaac realized his days were numbered. Instructing Esau to fix him a feast of wild game, Isaac prepared to give his patriarchal blessing to his beloved firstborn. (This tradition formally and legally bestowed huge material and emotional advantages on the oldest son.)

Rebekah happened to overhear this conversation. She leaped into action, convincing Jacob to join her in a brazen plan. Combining her exceptional culinary skills with Jacob's so-so acting ability, the mother-son duo managed to dupe Isaac into thinking Jacob was Esau.

For all her commendable qualities, Rebekah accomplished at least two things with this deceptive act. One, she secured the sought-after blessing for her precious Jacob. Two, she tore her family apart. Jacob ended up fleeing in fear. Esau bitterly moved away, and he married poorly.

THE TAKEAWAY

While it's natural for people to bond over shared interests, it's dangerous when parents play favorites. If you've been blessed to be a parent, ask yourself: Do I gravitate toward one kid? Do I make a bigger fuss over his or her accomplishments? Do I spend a disproportionate amount of time with him or her? Do I consistently take his or her side? Do I let that child come between my spouse and me?

Most adult siblings occasionally joke by saying things to each other like, "Mom always loved you best" or "You were always Dad's favorite." Make sure you don't give your children any basis in fact for such comments!

FOOD FOR THOUGHT

1. What do you admire most about Rebekah's life?

2. Were there instances of parental favoritism in your family of origin? If so, what were the consequences for you and your siblings?

3. If a close friend or family member were guilty of extreme parental favoritism, would you say something? Why or why not? If so, what would you say?

25

Rachel

BLESSED AND CURSED

"So Jacob worked seven years for Rachel, and they seemed like only a few days to him because of his love for her."
— *Genesis 29:20*

When Isaac became concerned about the neighborhood Canaanite girls stealing the heart of his youngest son, Jacob, he instructed Jacob to leave home: "Marry one of the daughters of Laban, your mother's brother" (Gen 28:2). So Jacob packed up and headed for Paddan-aram (his mom's hometown).

It was an emotional trip—leaving his parents, striking out on his own. On the way, Jacob stopped at Luz to get some shut-eye. During the night Yahweh himself appeared to Jacob in a dream, reiterating the promises he'd given years before to Jacob's grandfather Abraham. It was a good sign.

As Jacob neared his destination, he came to a well. Some local shepherds there were in the process of telling Jacob all about Laban when a gorgeous shepherdess—Laban's daughter Rachel—showed up with her flock. What happened next was like a scene from a romantic comedy. Jacob jumped up, watered Rachel's thirsty sheep, kissed his shocked cousin, and began to weep loudly. When he gathered himself, he told Rachel who he was. In a flash she was running home to tell her father the news (see Gen 29:1–12).

Jacob stuck around and started helping Laban out. When Laban became uncomfortable with all that free labor, he said to Jacob, "Tell me what your wages should be" (Gen 29:15). Jacob didn't even have to think. "I'll work for you seven years for your younger daughter Rachel" (29:18).

Seven years seems like a long time to us, but the "shapely and beautiful" Rachel was a catch, and Jacob was utterly smitten. Consequently the years "seemed like only a few days to him" (Gen 29:17–20).

However, on their wedding night Uncle Laban pulled a fast one. He gave Jacob his older, less attractive daughter, Leah. It sounds hard to believe, but whether due to darkness, an excess of veils, or perhaps too much wine at the reception, Jacob was none the wiser. In the bright light of morning, Jacob was justifiably ticked. He confronted Laban, calming down only when Laban agreed to give him Rachel in one week's time if Jacob would work for him seven more years. Jacob agreed.

Marriage is complicated; throw in an extra spouse, and things start getting really messy. Rachel was beloved, but childless. Leah, despite being unloved (see Gen 29:31), had several children. After watching her big sister produce four sons, Rachel became angry and desperate. She arranged for Jacob to have children by her servant girl, Bilhah, which resulted in the birth of two sons (see Gen 30:1–7). This started unhealthy competition between the sisters. Leah responded in kind, giving her handmaid, Zilpah, to Jacob. Soon, there were two *more* sons in this atypical family.

It wasn't until after Leah gave birth to two additional sons and a daughter that "God remembered Rachel. He listened to her and opened her womb. She conceived and bore a son, and said, 'God has taken away my shame'" (Gen 30:22–23). She named the boy Joseph, which means "may the LORD add another son to me" (30:24). The name was probably both a note of praise and a prayer.

Soon after the birth of Joseph, Jacob decided to take his family back to Canaan (see Gen 31:17–20). During the long journey, Jacob had a strange midnight wrestling match with God at the Jabbok River (see Gen 32:22–32). He also had a nerve-rattling reunion with his brother, Esau (see Gen 33:1–16). Rachel became pregnant again either during the family's sojourn in Succoth or their short stay at Shechem (see 33:17–18). It was after stopping to worship at Bethel, and then heading for Ephrath (Bethlehem), that Rachel went into severe labor (see 35:16).

Life was always so complicated for her. Her rare beauty. Her conniving father. Having to share her husband with an envious big sister. Infertility. And now this: giving birth in the middle of a trip in the middle of nowhere.

It was another boy. God had answered her prayer (see Gen 30:24). Realizing she wasn't going to see her newborn grow up, she named him Ben-oni, "son of my sorrow." Probably because he didn't want to think of Rachel's death every time he called his son, Jacob changed the boy's name to Benjamin. Then he buried the great love of his life.

THE TAKEAWAY

Sadly, Rachel spent much of her adult life frantically and foolishly trying to earn (or at least keep) the love of the man who was already head-over-heels crazy about her. *If I could just get pregnant; if I could only give him kids, then . . .*

She was completely secure, but she lived in insecurity. What a shame she couldn't rest in Jacob's love and enjoy his affection. In the same way, how many Christians scramble around—doing this and not doing that—in hopes of gaining just a tad bit more of God's favor?

Rachel reminds us that while life is complicated, God's love is not.

FOOD FOR THOUGHT

1. Why do you think God allowed all those polygamous marriages we read about in the Old Testament?

2. All trials are tough, but why is infertility especially devastating?

3. What are some practical ways we can address sibling rivalry?

29

Leah
THE UNLOVED SISTER

"When the LORD saw that Leah was unloved, He opened her womb; but Rachel was unable to conceive." — Genesis 29:31

Leah's father, Laban, was a piece of work. It wasn't easy being his oldest daughter. Her greater burden, however, was being the older sister of Rachel.

Everybody noticed Rachel. And why not? The Bible bluntly says she "was shapely and beautiful" (Gen 29:17); we can be sure family members, neighbors, and adolescent men raved nonstop about her. Meanwhile, poor Leah is described only as having "ordinary eyes." The idea is that next to her head-turning sister, Leah was all but invisible.

We don't have much information about the sisters' personalities or their childhood interactions. But when they were older, their sibling rivalry and insecurity came to a head. Jacob came for a visit. He was their cousin (his mom and their dad were sister and brother), who hailed from a wealthy family. Best of all, Jacob was single and looking to settle down.

Of course, the minute Jacob laid eyes on Rachel, he flipped head-over-heels in love with her. So much so that he agreed to serve Laban seven years for the right to make her his bride.

Watching that whole mushy relationship unfold was tough enough for Leah to stomach. But then on the wedding night, her father, well, pulled a Laban. Instead of giving Rachel to Jacob as promised, he sent Leah into the darkened "honeymoon suite."

The next morning Jacob was apoplectic. He confronted his wily old uncle/new father-in-law, securing a pledge to get his true love, Rachel, in seven more days if he'd agree to stick around and work seven more years.

When you try to put yourself in Leah's place, it just about kills your heart. To be the passed-over one, the ignored one, the undesirable one. But there she was. What could she do?

There were moments of grace and, dare we say it, sweet revenge. "When the LORD saw that Leah was unloved, He opened her womb" (Gen 29:31). In rapid-fire succession, she began having sons, even as Rachel found herself unable to conceive.

She named the first Reuben, saying, "The LORD has seen my affliction; surely my husband will love me now" (Gen 29:32). But apparently this momentous event failed to kindle any real affection in Jacob's heart, because upon the birth of her second son, she muttered, "The LORD heard that I am unloved" (29:33). A third birth revealed her lingering longing for love: "At last, my husband will become attached to me because I have borne three sons for him" (29:34). She marked the birth of her fourth son without referencing Jacob at all, saying only, "This time I will praise the

Lord" (29:35). Perhaps by this point she was resigned to the notion that she'd never be loved in the way she hoped. The pregnancies stopped.

But envy-fueled sibling rivalries don't easily die. A bitter Rachel decided to embrace the cultural practice of having a child via one's servant. She pushed her servant Bilhah on Jacob, resulting in two surrogate sons. Leah followed suit, which resulted in two more surrogate pregnancies of her own.

Even though she'd given Jacob six sons and a daughter, it wasn't enough. When Rachel finally conceived, it nearly killed Leah. Just as Leah feared, that newborn son, Joseph, the child of the favored wife, became the favored child of the next generation.

After all those maternal mentions, not much is said in Scripture about Leah. It seems that Rachel died first, while giving birth to her son Benjamin. No one can say for sure, but perhaps this altered the dynamic between Jacob and Leah.

Here is what we *do* know: when Jacob was on his death-bed and charging his sons, he mentioned the family plot "in the field of Machpelah near Mamre, in the land of Canaan" (Gen 49:30–31). It was the burial site for all the patriarchs of the faith. Abraham and Sarah were laid to rest there, and Isaac and Rebekah after them. Interestingly, Jacob had *Leah* buried there—*but not Rachel* (see Gen 35:19). Later, before he himself passed away, Jacob let it be known he wanted to be buried there, next to Leah.

It makes you wonder: perhaps the ordinary girl who just wanted to be wanted, who just wanted to be loved, was more wanted and more loved than she ever realized.

THE TAKEAWAY

We are tempted to say, "Poor girl!" when we think of Leah. But she was given the distinct privilege of being, with Rachel, one of the two women who is said to have "built the house of Israel" (Ruth 4:11).

One could even argue that Leah enjoyed greater honor than her younger, flashier sister (although that honor did not come until long after her death). It was Leah's son Levi who became the leader of Israel's priestly tribe. And it was Leah's son Judah, not one of Rachel's boys, who fathered the tribe from which the Messiah eventually came.

FOOD FOR THOUGHT

1. What five words would you use to describe Leah?

2. We tend to fixate on the things—abilities, attributes, resources, advantages—that we don't have. What are some of the blessings and opportunities you have been given, and how can you use them more effectively today?

3. What question would you like to ask Leah and why?

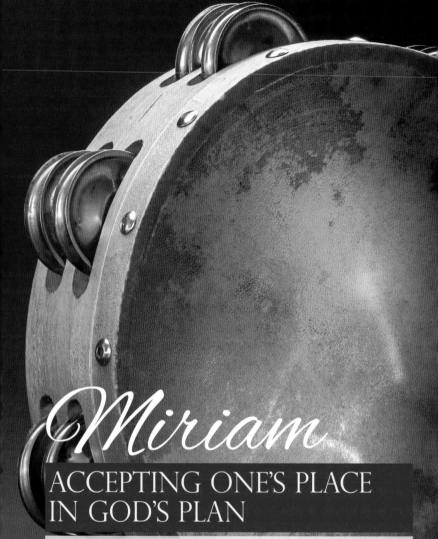

Miriam

ACCEPTING ONE'S PLACE IN GOD'S PLAN

"Then Miriam the prophetess, Aaron's sister, took a tambourine in her hand, and all the women followed her with their tambourines and danced." — *Exodus 15:20*

Miriam's greatest claim to fame wasn't that she was the daughter of Amram and Jochebed (see Num 26:59). It was that she was the sister of Moses.

Though she's not *named* in the famous story of the infant Moses being hidden in a basket, placed in the Nile River, then discovered and adopted by Pharaoh's daughter (see Exodus 2), she's almost certainly the "sister" mentioned there. In that incident, Miriam displayed both courage and resourcefulness. She proved herself to be the quintessential protective big sister.

The first time she is called by name in Scripture is when the children of Israel are celebrating their great deliverance from slavery in Egypt and safe passage through the Red Sea. Miriam is shown playing a prominent role on that great occasion, leading the fledgling nation (or at least the women) in worship (see Exod 15:20–21).

Over time, Miriam and her two brothers became a kind of "executive leadership team." The "baby"—that is, Moses—functioned like the CEO. From Miriam's perspective, Moses was the golden child. He was the one who survived when most of the other Hebrew boy babies didn't. He was the one who got to be raised by Egyptian royalty in luxury. He was the one who later was handpicked by God—who spoke to Moses out of a burning bush, no less!—to lead the Israelites to freedom. He was the one who got to meet regularly face to face with God on top of Mount Sinai (see Exod 33:11), receiving those tablets inscribed by the very finger of God. Sometimes the glory of his lengthy one-on-ones with the Almighty was so overwhelming that Moses literally shone for weeks after the fact.

Miriam's other brother, Aaron, acted as Moses' chief communications officer and VP of operations. Why Moses let him stay in that position after some of his boneheaded moves (see Exodus 32), Miriam couldn't understand. But at least she had the role of "prophetess" (Exod 15:20), meaning that, like her brother Moses, she too received revelations directly from the Almighty. She most likely comforted herself with the fact that they were every bit as valid and important as anything Moses ever spouted.

One day Aaron and Miriam finally had enough of playing second fiddle. They were sick of watching Moses get so much (literal) glory. When their frustration reached critical mass, they began to criticize their brother (see Num 12:1–12). They began with verbal attacks on his wife. But that was only a smoke screen. Very quickly, their real beef surfaced. "They said, 'Does the Lord speak only through Moses? Does He not also speak through us?' And the Lord heard it" (Num 12:2).

What happened next wasn't pretty. God called an emergency meeting of Israel's "executive council." When the three arrived at the tent of meeting, God told Moses he could wait outside. Then the Almighty called Miriam and Aaron inside and, in no uncertain terms, made it clear that Moses was *the* guy, *his* guy. And to underline this reality, Miriam left that meeting with a severe case of leprosy (probably because she was the instigator of this challenge to Moses' leadership).

It was Moses who stepped forward and pleaded with God to restore his sister to health. God agreed, but first he gave Miriam seven days to stare at her diseased skin and think about what she'd done (see Numbers 12). She seems to have learned some important life lessons from this incident: *Do with joy the thing God has called you to do. Be thankful for the opportunity to serve, and don't overstep your bounds. Refuse to compare yourself with others, resist the snare of envy, and don't sinfully criticize the leaders God has installed.*

Miriam isn't mentioned again in the biblical record until the time of her death (see Num 20:1).

THE TAKEAWAY

If you've ever tried to lead anything—a family, an organization, a project, or a company—you know that leadership is tricky business. It's lonely at the top. Every decision gets questioned and second-guessed. Everyone else always seems to have a better idea.

On the other side of things, it's easy to be a Monday morning quarterback and become critical of those who lead. Don't! Jesus calls us to humbly play the role he's given us instead of focusing on the shortcomings of others, wishing we had someone else's life or position, or grumbling about another person getting more attention and acclaim (see John 21:21–22).

If you want to fixate on something, let it be this question: "Am I being faithful to my own calling?" As Paul wrote, "Who are you to criticize another's household slave? Before his own Lord he stands or falls" (Rom 14:4).

FOOD FOR THOUGHT

1. Do you think everyone struggles at some point with envy of one form or another? Why is envy such a powerful sentiment?

2. Why do you think God's response to Miriam and Aaron's criticism of Moses was so severe?

3. Thinking about your own life, how can you become more content in the roles in which God has placed you? How can you become more supportive of a leader in your life?

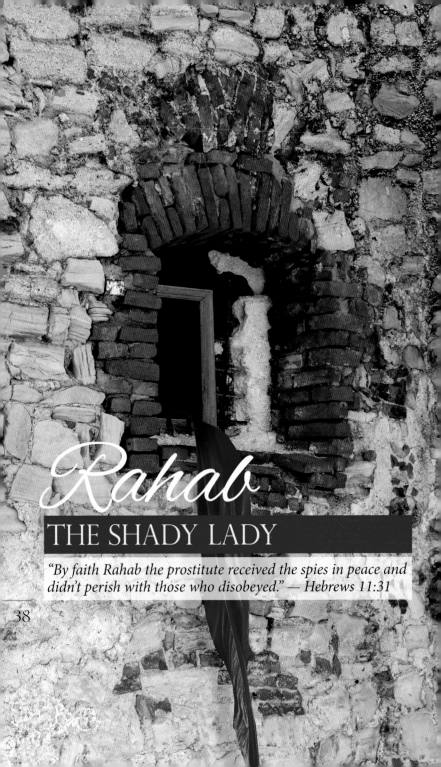

Rahab

THE SHADY LADY

"By faith Rahab the prostitute received the spies in peace and didn't perish with those who disobeyed." — Hebrews 11:31

There's no nice way to say it. Rahab was a harlot—in modern parlance, a hooker. At her home atop the wall that surrounded the bustling, ancient city of Jericho, Rahab took in strange men and gave out sexual favors.

Because of her prominent role in the story of Israel, a few prim and proper types have tried to improve Rahab's image by engaging in a bit of revisionist history. "Maybe," they've suggested, "she wasn't actually a 'lady of the night.' Perhaps she was only an 'innkeeper.'"

It's a nice try, a kind and understandable gesture; however, it can't change the truth that the Bible repeatedly calls Rahab a "prostitute." This is how the Bible introduces her when we first meet her in the book of Joshua (see Josh 2:1; 6:17). It's likely her home was less a motel and more a brothel.

Fully appreciating Rahab's remarkable story takes some historical and cultural background. After forty years of wandering in the desert east of Egypt and south of Canaan, the nation of Israel camped near the Jordan River, not far from Jericho. This was right along the edge of the territory said to be "flowing with milk and honey" (Exod 3:8; Num 14:8). It was this land the Lord—Yahweh, the God of the Israelites—had promised Abraham and his descendants centuries before.

Nervously watching the two to three *million* homeless refugees on their doorstep were the Canaanites, the current occupants of the land. "Canaanites" (Exod 3:8) is the generic name applied to the fierce, polytheistic tribes that lived in a patchwork of city-states stretching across the Holy Land all the way to the Mediterranean.

Like the rest of her neighbors, Rahab had heard all the stories: Yahweh's obliteration of the mighty Egyptians in liberating his people, his annihilation of lesser nations that dared to stand in Israel's way. Such anecdotes raised not only eyebrows but also heart rates and neck hairs! The Israelites themselves weren't much in the way of a fighting force, but their God was not to be trifled with. And suddenly there they were, massed on the border, clearly preparing to invade.

What do you suppose went through Rahab's mind when two Israelite men—sent by Joshua to scope out the city—knocked on her door? No one can say for sure, but clearly something shifted in the soul of this woman of ill repute.

Filled with holy fear and pierced by holy insight, Rahab swung into action. She first protected the spies (hiding them on her roof while telling the king's agents the strangers had come and gone). Second, she pleaded for mercy from the spies: "Now please swear to me by the Lord that you will also show kindness to my family, because I showed kindness to you. Give me a sure sign that you will spare the lives of my father, mother, brothers, sisters, and all who belong to them, and save us from death" (Josh 2:12–13).

The men consented to Rahab's request under these conditions: she would have to gather her family in her house during the invasion; she would need to hang a red rope from her window. This scarlet cord would signal to the conquering Israelites her whereabouts. If she did this, the spies assured, she and her loved ones would be unharmed. Rahab took the men at their word. After carrying out their instructions, she and her family were spared.

But the story doesn't end there. After Jericho's destruction, Rahab married an Israelite named Salmon. Together they had a child named Boaz, who was none other than the great-grandfather of King David! We know this because Rahab's name appears in the genealogy of Jesus Christ that begins the Gospel of Matthew (1:5). Two other times in the New Testament (see Heb 11:31; Jas 2:25), Rahab is mentioned and praised for her faith.

Seeing the name of a pagan prostitute listed in Scripture among spiritual icons like Abraham, Moses, and David is enough to make one wonder, "What's a bad girl like her doing here?" But when you know Rahab's story, the answer is obvious: *anyone* who responds in faith to God's gracious overtures can and will be saved.

THE TAKEAWAY

A product of Canaanite culture, Rahab had surely grown up a devotee of false gods. As a practitioner of the "world's oldest profession," her character was stained by immorality and dishonesty, her heart jaded and hardened by such a brutal existence.

The good news is that if God is willing and able to rescue someone like Rahab, he can redeem anyone! Her transformation shows that God is serious about "not wanting any to perish but all to come to repentance" (2 Pet 3:9). Rahab's experience underscores the gospel truth that we are not saved by our good works but by faith in who God is and what he has graciously done for us.

FOOD FOR THOUGHT

1. Does it trouble you or encourage you that God included a "shady lady" like Rahab in the ancestry of his Son, Jesus?

2. Who in your life right now would be most encouraged by the lesson of Rahab's life?

3. Rahab had heard stories of God's power, but the truth finally clicked—and her life changed—when she interacted with two of God's people who were engaged in God's mission. How involved are you in what God is doing in your family, church, and community?

Deborah

A WOMAN OF MANY TALENTS

"Deborah, a woman who was a prophetess and the wife of Lappidoth, was judging Israel at that time." — Judges 4:4

The name *Deborah* means "bee." The parents of Israel's fourth—and only female—judge could not have picked a more appropriate name for their daughter. Uncommonly gifted, this industrious woman grew up to accomplish extraordinary things with her life.

The Bible tells us she was married to a man named Lappidoth (though there's no overt mention of children). We also learn she was a prophetess, which means that like Miriam (see Exod 15:20) before her and Anna (see Luke 2:36) after her, Deborah regularly received divine revelation for her people.

Somewhere along the way, Deborah added the job of "judge" to her roles as wife and prophetess. This was during that lawless, rudderless time in Israel's history between Joshua and Saul, when the nation had no king (see Judg 17:6)—and even less of a sense of right and wrong. The judges apparently exercised some degree of legal authority. More often they served as military conquerors—securing freedom from outside oppressors and then presiding over periods of peace.

During her stint as judge, Deborah kept an "office" (literally a palm tree between Ramah and Bethel in the hill country of Ephraim; see Judg 4:5). There she likely shared God's truth, offered wise counsel, boosted national morale, and presided over disputes between her people in almost the same way a mom referees squabbles between her kids (see Judg 5:7).

It's safe to assume that juggling all these responsibilities and functions kept Deborah busy. But her shining moment was still to come. One day, at God's clear prompting, Deborah called Barak in and commanded him to take 10,000 men and attack the forces of Jabin, who were under the command of General Sisera. (Jabin was the Canaanite king who reigned in Hazor and who had been a thorn in the side of the children of Israel for more than two decades.)

Barak, due either to his own insecurity or to Deborah's great ability (or perhaps a bit of both), pleaded for her to accompany him into battle. "'I will go with you,' she said, 'but you will receive no honor on the road you are about to take, because the LORD will sell Sisera into a woman's hand.' So Deborah got up and went with Barak to Kedesh" (Judg 4:9).

Once the troops were in position on Mount Tabor, Deborah gave the signal, and Barak led the charge. Rushing down the mountainside, the ragtag Israelites routed the stronger, battle-tested Canaanites and their 900 iron chariots. Deliverance came largely because of Deborah's bold leadership—and, it seems, some timely, divine flooding (see Judg 5:21–22).

As per Deborah's prophecy, Sisera fled the battle and hid among the Kenites. While he snoozed, an Israelite sympathizer, a woman named Jael, took his life in a most inglorious manner (see Judg 4:17–21).

Following this overwhelming victory, Deborah composed a vivid, upbeat song (see Judg 5:2–31) to celebrate Israel's great deliverance. Who knew this busy prophetess, wife, and judge was also a gifted songwriter?

The "Song of Deborah" has long been praised for its literary qualities. Lyrically the song taps into all of Deborah's life experiences. It is God-centered, as we would expect from a spiritual leader or prophetess. It is full of the kinds of historical and military references that only a seasoned national leader (i.e., a "judge") would be able to describe. It is further filled with domestic imagery—concluding with the poignant picture of Sisera's mother looking out the window, waiting in vain for her son to return home from battle.

Mostly, Deborah's song is humble. It avoids any hint of self-congratulation, beginning with the words, "When the leaders lead in Israel, when the people volunteer, praise the Lord." In other words, victory is a team effort and ultimately the work of the Lord.

While the nation looked on, Deborah performed her composition with Barak (see Judg 5:1). The fact that we still have the song suggests it was quite a hit in Israel.

Following these events, Israel enjoyed forty years of peace and quiet (see Judg 5:31). Surely Deborah kept busy to the end of her days.

THE TAKEAWAY

One conclusion we can draw from the life of Deborah is that certain people are given rare leadership ability. God graces each one of us with unique abilities and one-of-a-kind opportunities. In certain situations we are called to lead. In other settings we are expected to volunteer, to follow. This much we know: we are all called by God to play a role. We each have a part.

When, like Barak, we doubt the promise of God and shrink back, we miss out on the full experience of being used by God. When, like Deborah, we step forward and bravely exercise our gifts, we end up having a huge impact.

Deborah teaches us to busy ourselves in doing all the things God has given us to do, all for his glory.

FOOD FOR THOUGHT

1. What are the various roles you play in life?

2. What do others say are your gifts, special talents, and unique abilities?

3. Are there situations in your life in which you feel nudged to engage but question whether you could really make a difference? If so, what are they? What keeps you from stepping out?

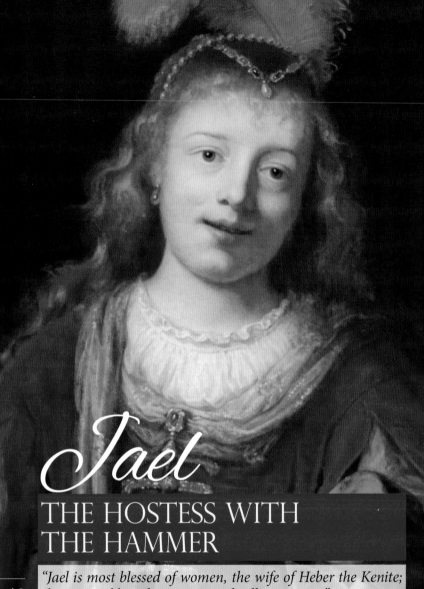

Jael

THE HOSTESS WITH THE HAMMER

"Jael is most blessed of women, the wife of Heber the Kenite;
she is most blessed among tent-dwelling women."
— Judges 5:24

J ael is the Bible character who sparks one-liners about "splitting head-aches." She's the woman who jokesters like to refer to as "an expert at helping men 'get things through their thick skulls!'" But we are getting ahead of ourselves. A bit of context is needed.

Following the Israelites' crossing of the Jordan River, Israel's campaign to conquer and settle the promised land got off to a spectacular start. But over time, for multiple reasons, the effort sputtered and lost steam. Taking over a country is trying, not to mention tiring.

By Joshua's final days, the people of God had pretty much given up attempting to squash the pockets of Canaanite resistance that were popping up left and right. After Joshua went to glory, the nation went off the rails.

It wasn't long before the Angel of the Lord showed up and announced the dire consequences of Israel's slide into sin: "I will not drive out these people before you. They will be thorns in your sides, and their gods will be a trap for you" (Judg 2:3).

These events ushered in an extremely dark period in Israel's history. The chronicler of that era (likely the prophet Samuel), summed up this chaotic, lawless period with these chilling words: "In those days there was no king in Israel; *everyone did whatever he wanted*" (Judg 21:25, emphasis added).

Over 300 years, a grim cycle repeated itself time and again. The Israelites' collective idolatry would eventually become so grievous that God would allow an enemy nation to subjugate his people. This would inevitably result in the people of God crying out to God. In response, God would graciously provide deliverance through either a great warrior like Samson (see Judges 13–16), a timid leader like Gideon (see Judges 6–8), or an unlikely hero like Deborah (see Judges 4–5). These military deliverers were known as the "judges" (Judg 2:16).

Jael lived during the years when Deborah, Israel's only female judge, was leading a spirited effort to free her people from Jabin, an oppressive Canaanite king. Jael was married to a Kenite man named Heber.

The two were minding their own business, camping near Kedesh by the oak tree of Zaanannim (see Judg 4:11), when the Israelite-Canaanite conflict came to a bloody culmination nearby. Barak (the military commander of Israel) led 10,000 troops down Mount Tabor. They engaged the Canaanite army that was under the command of Sisera (Jabin's top general; see Judg 4:1–10). With God's help, the Israelites overwhelmed the Canaanites, killing every single soldier and chariot-eer (see Judg 4:16).

All except for Sisera. He escaped somehow and fled, ending up at Jael's front door. He assumed he would be safe there, and why not? His boss, King Jabin, and the Kenite people enjoyed a cordial relationship (see Judg 4:17). It was a terrible miscalculation on Sisera's part.

Under the pretense of providing shelter and showing hospitality, Jael took Sisera into her tent. She hid the scared, exhausted commander, offered him milk to drink, and gave him a place to sleep. When he dozed off, she reached for her hammer. The last thing that ever went through Sisera's mind was one very large tent peg (see Judg 4:17–21).

We don't know what possessed Jael to violate all protocols of hospitality and commit such a treacherous act. Perhaps she regarded the Kenites' family connection to Israel (i.e., the Kenites were descendants of Hobab [aka Jethro], the father-in-law of Moses; see Judg 4:11) as more binding than any newer political alliance. Or maybe she sensed in the stunning victory of the Israelites over the superior Canaanites proof that Yahweh was the one true God. Whatever the case, when Sisera began to snore, Jael struck.

Later, Deborah, the leader of Israel, commemorated Jael's coldly courageous act in a song (see Judg 5:24). Jael is never mentioned again in Scripture, though it's not hard to imagine that after these events she was a frequent topic of conversation around dinner tables for quite some time.

THE TAKEAWAY

This is one of those dark passages of Scripture that shocks us with its graphic nature. What is there to emulate from a woman who tricked a vulnerable army commander and then took his life in such a cold-blooded manner? Maybe only this: Jael cast her lot with God, his people, and his purposes.

During the Civil War, a Northern minister allegedly said to Abraham Lincoln that he "hoped the Lord was on the Union's side." The president responded, "I am not at all concerned about that. . . . But it is my constant anxiety and prayer that I and this nation should be on the Lord's side."

Living in an era when most people, most of the time, do pretty much whatever they feel like doing, striving to be on the Lord's side is a great strategy for life.

FOOD FOR THOUGHT

1. When you read a biblical story like Jael's, what kinds of questions does it raise in your heart?

2. It's often said that desperate times call for desperate measures. Is that a good explanation for this bloody series of events?

3. What scary or difficult thing are you facing in your life right now, and what courageous choice do you need to make?

Delilah

USED TO BEING USED

"Some time later, [Samson] fell in love with a woman named Delilah, who lived in the Sorek Valley." — Judges 16:4

E ven though it's a pretty name, not too many parents name their baby daughters *Delilah*. In Judges 16, where we find the story of the original Delilah, we discover why.

Delilah's nationality, family background, and hometown are all mysteries. Most scholars suspect she was a Philistine. Others speculate she was a prostitute at a pagan temple. All we know for sure is that she lived somewhere in the valley of Sorek and that her name has come to symbolize treacherous sensuality.

Delilah lived during the twenty-year period when the mighty Samson was being used by God to deliver Israel from Philistine oppression (see Judg 13:1–16:31). Whenever God's Spirit came upon Samson, he engaged in the sorts of exploits only comic book heroes are said to do. He tore roaring lions apart with his bare hands. He wiped out whole gangs of Philistines—from 30 to 1,000 soldiers at a time. Samson's God-given strength was his claim to fame.

Sadly, his unbridled sexual appetite was Samson's claim to *shame*. Multiple times in the biblical record we see the moral weakness of this physically strong servant of God. On one occasion, a Philistine woman from Timnah caught Samson's eye. The fact that she was a pagan was irrelevant to him—all he cared about was that she was attractive. "Get her for me as a wife," he told his father (Judg 14:2). In Gaza he slept with a prostitute (see 16:1). Moving on from her, he met Delilah (see 16:4). Did he simply have a high capacity for love? Or was he driven by fleshly desires?

Whatever the true nature of Samson's desire for Delilah, it was intense. When word got out that he and she were an item, Samson's private life and professional life became dangerously intertwined. "The Philistine leaders went to [Delilah] and said, 'Persuade [Samson] to tell you where his great strength comes from, so we can overpower him, tie him up, and make him helpless. Each of us will then give you 1,100 pieces of silver'" (Judg 16:5).

Delilah pounced at this lucrative offer like a frog snatching a bug. Summoning all her considerable female wiles, she immediately began flirting and cajoling and wheedling. She pulled out all the stops to get Samson to reveal the secret behind his unearthly power.

Time and again he toyed with her, providing misleading answers. Time and again, she leaked this bad information to her Philistine clients. With each bungled attempt by the Philistines to capture Samson, Delilah became increasingly pouty. Dollar signs in her eyes, the temptress ratcheted up the pressure. She went for the kill:

"How can you say, 'I love you,'" she told him, "when your heart is not with me? This is the third time you have mocked me and not told me what makes your strength so great!"

Because she nagged him day after day and pleaded with him until she wore him out, he told her the whole truth and said to her, "My hair has never been cut, because I am a Nazirite to God from birth. If I am shaved, my strength will leave me, and I will become weak and be like any other man."

When Delilah realized that he had told her the whole truth, she sent this message to the Philistine leaders: "Come one more time, for he has told me the whole truth." The Philistine leaders came to her and brought the money with them. (Judg 16:15–18)

Perhaps you know the end of the story. When Samson was sleeping (either drunk from wine or love, or maybe both), Delilah saw to it that his head was shaved.

Then, while she counted her bags of silver, the Philistines tied up the impotent Samson, poked out his eyes, and led him away. In death he would have one last glorious victory over Israel's enemy (see Judg 16:23–30), but not before he suffered great humiliation.

As far as the sneaky, sultry Delilah, she is never heard from again.

THE TAKEAWAY

Don't you wonder about Delilah's life? About her past and experience with men? Did she learn early on that external beauty can sometimes be more of a curse than it is a blessing? Was she ever married? Was she a prostitute? The daughter of a prostitute?

And what about Delilah's relationship with Samson? Did she get her hopes up at the beginning and think, even fleetingly, *Maybe this time it'll be different. After all, he's a servant of the Holy One of Israel. Surely he'll treat me right.* Did she turn on Samson when his "love" turned out to be "lust"?

It's dangerous to speculate where the Bible is silent, but it sure does seem like Delilah was a woman who was used to being used. Endure that for very long and it's not hard to embrace a philosophy that says, "Take advantage of others before they take advantage of you."

FOOD FOR THOUGHT

1. What are your biggest questions about this mysterious woman named Delilah?

2. What do Samson and Delilah's conversations/interactions reveal about male-female relationships?

3. If you met and befriended a woman with a background like Delilah's, what encouragement would you give her? How does the gospel of Jesus speak to someone with deep hurt and pain?

53

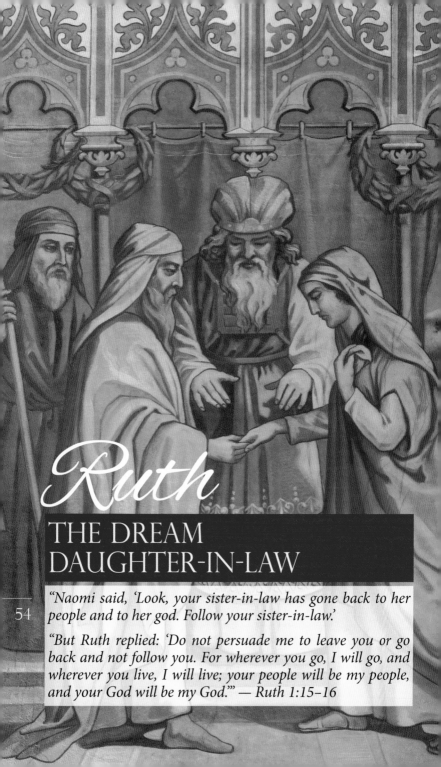

Ruth

THE DREAM DAUGHTER-IN-LAW

"Naomi said, 'Look, your sister-in-law has gone back to her people and to her god. Follow your sister-in-law.'

"But Ruth replied: 'Do not persuade me to leave you or go back and not follow you. For wherever you go, I will go, and wherever you live, I will live; your people will be my people, and your God will be my God.'" — Ruth 1:15–16

W e all have someone in our lives with whom a close relationship seems impossible. Maybe it's a sibling, a parent, a child, or even a spouse. For whatever reasons, we just can't seem to get along. Outside of our families, most of us have other difficult relationships—with bosses, neighbors, business associates, coworkers, clients.

In the Old Testament book of Ruth, we meet a couple of women who model an extraordinary, highly unlikely relationship. They're in-laws (Ruth married one of Naomi's two sons), and by the fifth verse of the book, both women are widows.

There are a myriad of reasons why these two women never should have hit it off. They faced some or all of the following obstacles:

- *The in-law problem.* Tension between a mother-in-law and daughter-in-law is a real phenomenon in every culture and era.

- *Age difference.* The generation gap is also real in every culture and era.

- *Cultural differences.* Naomi was an Israelite; Ruth was a Moabite.

- *Religious barriers.* Ruth possibly grew up worshiping the god Chemosh. This would have been reprehensible to a monotheistic Israelite like Naomi.

- *Class struggles.* Some scholars think the description of Naomi's family as "Ephrathites" (Ruth 1:2) means they had been part of Jerusalem's high society. If Ruth was from the working class, you can imagine the potential for conflict.

- *Economic hardship.* Life for widows is rough in any culture. It was especially difficult then. Many ended up begging or turning to prostitution.

Yet with all those strikes against them, Ruth and Naomi forged a close and loving relationship. How?

Mostly what sticks out is Ruth's unusual commitment: "Wherever you go, I will go, and wherever you live, I will live; your people will be my people, and your God will be my God" (Ruth 1:16). This classic statement, so often quoted at weddings, was originally made by a daughter-in-law to her mother-in-law. Isn't that ironic? Many people do everything they possibly can to avoid their in-laws even when their spouses are alive! But here is a woman who committed herself irrevocably to her mother-in-law after her husband was dead and buried. It is this kind of head-scratching commitment that can turn potentially bad relationships into blessed ones.

The unselfishness Ruth and Naomi showed in looking out for one other is admirable (see Ruth 1:7–14; 2:18). At crucial moments, each one's greatest concern was not "What do *I* need or want?" but "What would be best for *you*?" Such a selfless attitude led to acts of kindness. At one point Ruth announced she would gather grain for the two of them (see Ruth 2:2). It's an act of service that's all the more amazing when you realize it followed right on the heels of Naomi's extreme insensitivity toward Ruth (see Ruth 1:19–21). Ruth had just pledged her life-long commitment to Naomi and accompanied her back to Bethlehem. In response, Naomi moaned about how empty and bitter her life was. Ruth might have thought, "Thanks a lot! What am I? Chopped liver?" But she was understanding and relentlessly kind. The next day she was out gathering food for her mother-in-law.

In the great story of God, the sparkling behavior of the Moabite Ruth is meant to contrast with the faithlessness of the Israelite people. Ruth is blessed because of her actions. In her new home of Israel she became the wife of Boaz, the great-grandmother of King David, and part of the lineage of Christ. On an interpersonal level, her life shows how it's possible to build relational bridges instead of relational walls.

THE TAKEAWAY

Think about a difficult relationship in your own life. Maybe you've gotten off to a bad start. Here's the good news: the gospel is all about grace and new beginnings. If you're at fault, own it. Ask for forgiveness. If the person with whom you are trying to relate is a believer, you have every reason to hope for a deeper relationship. The same Holy Spirit indwells you both.

If your difficult relationship is complicated by the fact that the other person is not a follower of Christ, don't despair. Apologize sincerely for any wrong words or actions. Then model what it means to know God. Talk about what God is doing in your life—not in a pushy, preachy way, but humbly and naturally. Pray fervently. Then wait for the Spirit to work.

Difficult relationships work best when both people are committed to Christ. But there can also be movement and growth even if only one of the parties trusts God and determines to do the right thing. Be committed, selfless, and kind—just like Ruth!

FOOD FOR THOUGHT

1. What would have caused Ruth to leave her family (and any practical hope of ever remarrying) to follow her bitter mother-in-law to a new country?

2. Why are in-law relationships so tricky and so rarely positive?

3. As you think about the relationships in your life, which one do you feel most compelled to work on right now? Why?

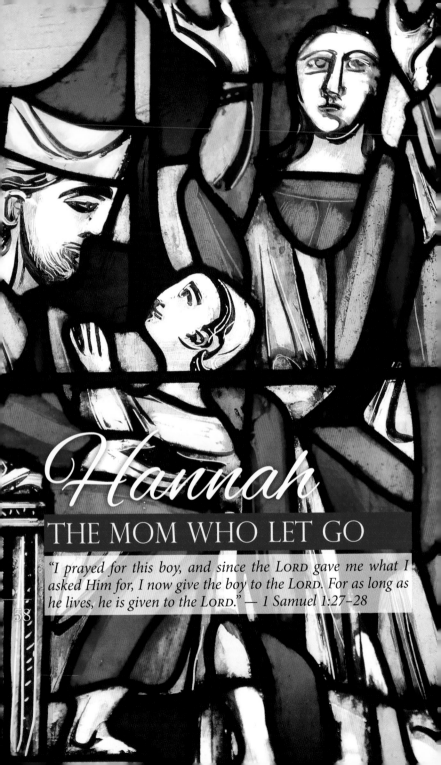

Hannah
THE MOM WHO LET GO

"I prayed for this boy, and since the Lord gave me what I asked Him for, I now give the boy to the Lord. For as long as he lives, he is given to the Lord." — *1 Samuel 1:27–28*

58

In the Old Testament book of 1 Samuel, we meet a woman named Hannah. She was married to a man named Elkanah, of the tribe of Ephraim. They lived in the hill country, in a little town with a big name—Ramathaim-zophim.

As was common in that culture, Elkanah had a second wife—Peninnah. And, as is usually the case in multiple marriages, Elkanah's home was full of tension and angst.

Hannah means "grace." Perhaps because of Elkanah's love—he favored her over Peninnah (see 1 Sam 1:4–5)—Hannah felt graced much of the time. It's not a stretch, however, to surmise that every time Hannah saw the empty crib in her empty nursery, she felt cursed. For whatever reason, she was barren. Peninnah, meanwhile, had multiple children. As we might expect, these women became fierce rivals (1:6).

Kids can become a kind of currency or status symbol. This is not a new phenomenon. Children (in quantity or quality) can become a measuring stick, a way of keeping score. Peninnah, likely out of her woundedness and bitterness, gloated over her fertility. She actually took to taunting her "sister wife," which was especially hurtful and humiliating to Hannah on the annual trips to Shiloh, where Elkanah's not-so-happy family worshiped, offered sacrifices, and feasted before the Lord.

One year Hannah couldn't take it anymore. She melted down, excusing herself from the sacrificial feast. Going back over to the tabernacle, she poured out her heart to God. In between her great, racking sobs, Hannah made a deal with God—or at least a vow to him. She swore that if he would give her a son, she would devote the boy to God's service. (Think of an ancient Jewish boarding school arrangement.) He would live a consecrated, alcohol-free life as a Nazirite.

As Hannah blubbered loudly and prayed fervently but silently, Eli the priest watched with dismay. Deciding this worked-up woman must have had a couple of glasses of wine too many at the feast, he scolded her. "No, my lord," responded Hannah, insisting she wasn't inebriated. "I am a woman with a broken heart. . . . Don't think of me as a wicked woman; I've been praying from the depth of my anguish and resentment" (1 Sam 1:15–16).

Satisfied she was sad, not sauced, Eli blessed her: "Go in peace, and may the God of Israel grant the petition you've requested from Him" (1 Sam 1:17). Sure enough, when she returned home Hannah conceived at long last. In accordance with the desires of her heart, she gave birth to a son. She named him Samuel, which means "God has heard."

After she weaned young Samuel, Hannah made good on her vow. She and her husband gathered up the boy, who was probably only four or five, and made the trek back to Shiloh. There they offered sacrifices to God and found Eli. Hannah told him the story of how God answered her prayer: "'Please, my lord,' she said, 'as sure as you live, my lord, I am the woman who stood here beside you praying to the LORD. I prayed for this boy, and since the LORD gave me what I asked Him for, I now give the boy to the LORD. For as long as he lives, he is given to the LORD'" (1 Sam 1:26–28).

Leaving their young son with Eli so that he might begin his religious training, the couple departed. Then, like a prophetess, filled with the Holy Spirit, Hannah worshiped God with a beautiful prayer (see 1 Sam 2:1–10).

God wasn't done "gracing" the woman whose name means "grace." He later gave her five other children: three sons and two daughters (see 1 Sam 2:21). But it was her firstborn, Samuel, who became a great prophet, a beloved and respected spiritual leader, and an influential adviser to Israel's kings.

THE TAKEAWAY

There are so many lessons in the story of Hannah: God's goodness and grace to his people, the wisdom of sticking to the biblical ideal for marriage (i.e., one man and one woman for life), the power of prayer, the importance of kindness, the blessings that come from living with integrity.

But perhaps the biggest reminder from Hannah's life is the truth that God's *blessings* are more technically *loans*. Our stuff isn't really "our" stuff. Our kids aren't really "our" kids. The teaching of Scripture is that God owns everything in all the world (see Deut 10:14; Pss 24:1; 50:12). This makes us stewards or caretakers or managers. So when we give back to God, we're really only giving him what's already his in the first place.

Whether in our finances, careers, or parenting, our goal should always be God's greater glory, not our own.

FOOD FOR THOUGHT

1. Can you think of some specific ways we live vicariously through our children?

2. In what ways do you struggle with viewing God as the owner of all you have?

3. What are the unique tensions for parents and children when a child feels a pull toward some kind of full-time Christian ministry?

Abigail

MARRIED TO A FOOL

"Abigail . . . was intelligent and beautiful, but [her husband] was harsh and evil in his dealings." — 1 Samuel 25:3

The story of Abigail is found primarily in 1 Samuel 25. We learn that she was "intelligent and beautiful" (v. 3) and married to "a very rich man" (v. 2). They lived in Maon, and he commuted to work—he was in the sheep and goat business—in Carmel. If that's all we knew, we'd conclude Abigail was beyond blessed. To be attractive *and* smart *and* well-to-do? Living in the suburbs? Who wouldn't want all that?

But, alas, things are not always what they seem on the surface. There's a lot more to Abigail's story, and much of it wasn't pretty.

Her wealthy husband's name was Nabal, which means "fool." Since it's hard to imagine a parent giving their newborn such a horrible name, some feel *Nabal* was simply a nickname. After all, the Bible *does* go on to describe him as one who "was harsh and evil in his dealings" (1 Sam 25:3).

With that kind of reputation, it's not hard to imagine that clients and neighbors pinned this moniker on him. Whatever the source of the name, there's this question: If Nabal was less than kind in his business affairs, why should we imagine he was any different at home? And you have to wonder something else: What's a sharp girl like Abigail doing with a man like this?

We wouldn't even know about this couple if it weren't for a fateful encounter with David, Israel's most famous warrior and king-in-waiting. It unfolded like this: Nabal happened to be shearing some sheep close to where David and his men were camped. When David heard Nabal was in the neighborhood, he sent his men to ask a favor. His request went something like this: "Food is kind of scarce out here in the wilderness. Do you think in exchange for the way we've always treated you with respect (and even protected you), you might be willing to give my hungry band a meal?"

Nabal not only yelled at David's men, scoffing at their request, but also heaped insults on them as they departed. In just a few foolish moments, Nabal violated every written and unwritten rule of Middle Eastern hospitality.

When David's men reported this humiliating exchange, David was livid. "He said to his men 'All of you, put on your swords!'" (1 Sam 25:13).

Things could have and would have gotten ugly, but thankfully one of Nabal's workers slipped away and brought Abigail into the loop. Then he blurted out the ugly truth about Nabal (the truth Abigail knew all too well from years of painful experience): "He is such a worthless fool nobody can talk to him!" (1 Sam 25:17).

The intelligent, beautiful, and now extremely frightened Abigail swung into action. She quickly threw together a huge and lovely picnic lunch: mutton, bread, and wine, with raisins and figs for dessert. Sending this feast ahead via some of her male servants, Abigail then got ready herself and went to see if she could avert a bloodbath.

She intercepted David just in time. Falling humbly at his feet, Abigail acknowledged her husband's foolish arrogance. Then, almost in the same breath, she pleaded for David to forgive and show mercy. It was a very reasoned appeal, a moving petition. In effect, she entreated David not to descend to the level of her "worthless" husband.

David's heart was pierced by Abigail's wise warning. He called off his attack.

Meanwhile, Abigail returned home to find her obnoxious husband stuffing his face and drunk out of his mind. He was blissfully oblivious to how close he'd come that very day to meeting his Maker. "In the morning when Nabal sobered up, his wife told him about these events" (1 Sam 25:37). He had a stroke and died ten days later.

After hearing about Nabal's death, David wasted no time sending one of his men to Abigail to broach the subject of marriage. Would this gracious, quick-thinking woman, who had demonstrated she was just as attractive inside as she was gorgeous on the outside, be interested in becoming David's wife? Abigail, not exactly grief-stricken, said yes without hesitation.

THE TAKEAWAY

Abigail reminds us that nobody has it all together. The perfect, ideal life is an imaginary life. It doesn't exist. Even the people who seem so put together have junk, baggage, struggles, and problems. As we ponder Abigail's story, two warnings are in order.

First, be careful about comparing yourself with others and wishing you had someone else's life. You don't really know what goes on in the hearts and homes of other people. There's undisclosed drama behind every face.

Second, be kind. As the old saying reminds us, "Everyone we meet is fighting a great battle." Unless we're like Nabal, we will always look back and regret being harsh. We will never regret showing mercy and being compassionate toward others.

FOOD FOR THOUGHT

1. Between looks, money, and intelligence, which would you say is the greatest blessing and which is the greatest curse? Why?

2. What do you admire most about Abigail? Least?

3. What counsel would you give a friend in Abigail's situation (i.e., married to a foolish, harsh person)?

Michal

A CRAZY, COMPLICATED LIFE

"As the ark of the LORD was entering the city of David, Saul's daughter Michal looked down from the window and saw King David leaping and dancing before the LORD, and she despised him in her heart." — 2 Samuel 6:16

I f we could interview Michal—the daughter of Saul and first wife of David—what might she say about her crazy, complicated life?

We would have to ask about her experience of being "a royal," the youngest of King Saul's five children (see 1 Sam 14:49). No doubt she could regale us with jaw-dropping stories of wealth and privilege.

We would inquire about the day she, like everyone else in Israel, became fixated on the big story coming out of the Elah Valley. There, a handsome young shepherd, to everyone's astonishment, had killed and beheaded the Philistine giant Goliath (see 1 Samuel 17). In a flash, *David* was a household name. Even as Michal's father was making the kid from Bethlehem a commander in his elite special forces unit, her big brother Jonathan was declaring the youthful giant killer his closest friend!

Surely Michal could reminisce about what it was like to join swooning females from all over Israel in singing about David's exploits (see 1 Sam 18:6–9). Next she'd tell us about how she held her breath the day her father tried to arrange a marriage between the heartthrob David and her big sister Merab (and the immense relief she felt when David declined).

There are so many other questions we would ask: Was David just a schoolgirl crush, or was he the great love of Michal's life? Did she realize her dad was merely trying to eliminate a potential rival when he offered David her hand in marriage (setting the dowry at 100 dead Philistines)? How special did she feel when she learned that David rushed out and killed *twice* that number of enemy troops?

We would inquire about what it was like for Michal to watch her father's jealousy of her new husband's popularity degenerate into suspicious paranoia, then into a murderous rage. "Tell us about the night you helped David escape from your father's henchmen," we would say (see 1 Sam 19:11–17).

The Bible doesn't say much about Michal's next few years, focusing instead on David's life as a fugitive for a decade or more. What was that like for Michal, watching her own father put a bounty on her husband's head? How did she deal with the dysfunction of it all, the separation and uncertainty? In effect, she became the widow of a living husband. How does one grieve such a thing?

And then the shock of being given by her father to another man, "Palti son of Laish, who was from Gallim" (1 Sam 25:44). Did Michal see that coming? Did she have any say in it? What was that marriage like? What was he like? Did Michal love him? (He sure seemed crazy about her.)

Maybe if it weren't too painful, Michal would speak about the wartime deaths of her father and brothers (see 1 Samuel 31). Perhaps we could get her to open up about the bizarre experience of being reclaimed by David after all those years apart, about the terrible pain of having to watch and listen to Palti weeping bitterly, calling her name as she walked out of his life.

As awkward as it would be, we'd have to bring up the famous incident when the ark of the covenant was being returned to Jerusalem. David was positively euphoric—so much so he began to dance wildly and unashamedly before the Lord. The prophet Samuel records, however, that as Michal watched David in those moments, "she despised him in her heart" (2 Sam 6:14–23). Why such contempt, such scorn? Where did such strong feelings come from?

Finally, would we be right in assuming that Michal's emotion in that moment was about much, much more than that moment?

THE TAKEAWAY

When it comes to a life punctuated by grief, Michal's not in a league of her own. Most people have plenty of disappointing and painful experiences. Who hasn't seen their life take a sudden, unexpected turn? The big dilemma is how to navigate such bitter events without becoming bitter yourself.

The brief, biblical portrait of Michal is of a brave, outspoken, resilient woman. On matters of faith, however, the Bible paints a less-than-encouraging picture. Though

Michal was clearly smitten with David, her love for Yahweh was suspect. There are references to idolatry (see 1 Sam 19:11–17). And her reaction to David's unabashed worship is troubling. What a shame that Michal wasn't able to see past David's many domestic shortcomings to the God he so adored.

The God who eventually turned David's bitter existence into a dance party could have done the same for Michal. He is glad to do that for anyone who humbly asks.

FOOD FOR THOUGHT

1. Which of Michal's hard life experiences (note: she also died childless; see 2 Sam 6:23) would have been most difficult to endure? Why?

2. What do you think prompted Michal's strong reaction to David's exuberant celebration?

3. Can you think of any situations in which you fight the tendency to be bitter (such as unfulfilled dreams or trials entering your life)? What is your plan to avoid becoming angry at God or others?

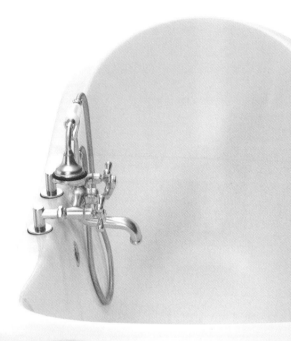

Bathsheba

THE VERY BEAUTIFUL WOMAN WITH THE VERY TRAGIC LIFE

"One evening David got up from his bed and strolled around on the roof of the palace. From the roof he saw a woman bathing—a very beautiful woman. So David sent someone to inquire about her, and he reported, 'This is Bathsheba, daughter of Eliam and wife of Uriah the Hittite.'" — *2 Samuel 11:2–3*

T here are a number of cautionary tales in the Bible, but few are as seamy and sad as this one.

Looking down on the city of Jerusalem from atop his royal palace one fine spring evening, Israel's King David spotted a fine young woman. She wasn't merely attractive; she was "very beautiful." And, of all the things she might have been doing, she was bathing.

The already-married David should have ordered some shutters. Instead he ordered an aide to find out the woman's identity. Even after he learned Bathsheba was Mrs. Uriah—that is, the wife of one of his most decorated military leaders (see 1 Chr 11:41)—David sent for her. She made her way over to the palace. And after a night of passion, Bathsheba found herself pregnant.

She notified the king. David immediately went into frantic, damage control mode. He tried to cover up his inexcusable behavior by ordering Uriah home from the front. He met with him and pretended to care about his well-being. Next he casually suggested Uriah go home and spend time with his wife. Uriah wouldn't hear of it, as he was unwilling to selfishly enjoy luxury and pleasure while his fellow soldiers were camped on a battlefield. Even when "David got him drunk" (2 Sam 11:13), Uriah refused to go home.

David panicked. The king after God's heart made an extremely horrible decision: he would add the heinous crime of murder to his hideous sin of adultery. He wrote a letter to his top general that read, "Put Uriah at the front of the fiercest fighting, then withdraw from him so that he is struck down and dies" (2 Sam 11:15).

David's plan seemed to work like a charm. Uriah was killed in the battle. After his funeral and an appropriate time of mourning (and probably just before Bathsheba got her "baby bump"), David married Uriah's young widow and moved her into the royal palace. She gave birth to David's child, a son. And perhaps for a brief time David thought maybe he'd managed to cover up his greatest scandal.

Not even close.

God sent the prophet Nathan to confront the wayward king with his sin. After rebuking David, but before leaving his presence, the bold Nathan also foretold of grim, irreversible consequences: long-term unceasing turmoil within David's family. And in the short term? The death of the newborn child.

Bathsheba (also known as Bath-shua; 1 Chr 3:5) pulled out her black dress again. Another funeral. Another round of grief. She eventually gave David four more sons—most notably Solomon—to go along with the many other sons he fathered by at least six other wives and an untold number of concubines (see 1 Chr 3:1–9).

If we only glance at Bathsheba, we might feel envious. All that beauty. All that privilege. Married to Israel's greatest king. The mother of the wisest man on earth, who she shrewdly helped rise to the throne.

But when we take a closer look, we see a lifetime of tragedy. Beyond the pain of saying goodbye to her husband Uriah, burying her infant son, and living as one of David's many wives and numerous concubines, Bathsheba's life was in constant crisis. She had to stand by and watch as her big, new dysfunctional family dealt with sibling rape and murder (see 2 Samuel 13). She had to flee the royal palace when Absalom, one of her stepsons, attempted a coup (see 2 Samuel 15). When she tried to help broker a marriage for Adonijah, one of her stepsons, her efforts led to his execution (see 1 Kgs 2:13–25).

All that makes one wonder how many times Bathsheba thought back to the ill-fated spring evening she took a rooftop bath and wished for a do over.

THE TAKEAWAY

The David and Bathsheba affair raises so many questions. Don't you wish you could personally interview this couple?

David, why weren't you with your troops? After all, it was springtime, "when kings march out to war" (2 Sam 11:1). Why were you lolling around the palace in your pajamas in the early evening? We get that you maybe

couldn't help seeing a naked woman in plain view, but why did you inquire as to her identity? More importantly, why did you send for her? You already had other wives—why did you feel the need, much less the freedom, to take another man's wife?

And Bathsheba, surely you had to know your "bathtub" was visible from the king's palace. Couldn't you have been more modest? Why did you go when the king's messengers knocked on your door? Did you do it because you were scared? Or were you unhappy? Lonely? How could you live with the man who ordered the death of your husband—or did you never know that fact?

What were you thinking?

FOOD FOR THOUGHT

1. Is Bathsheba a sympathetic character to you? Why or why not?

2. What question would you want to ask Bathsheba and/or David?

3. As you think about Bathsheba's story, what would you say is the lesson from her life?

Jezebel

HOW NOT TO LIVE YOUR LIFE

"Still, there was no one like Ahab, who devoted himself to do what was evil in the LORD's sight, because his wife Jezebel incited him." — 1 Kings 21:25

Ⅰt's hard to find nice things to say about the woman whose name has become synonymous for being shameless, brazen, and morally bankrupt.

Jezebel came *from* royalty—her father was Ethbaal, a Phoenician king. She also married *into* royalty—her husband, Ahab, was the king of the ten tribes that made up the northern kingdom of Israel (see 1 Kgs 16:29–33).

That an Israelite king would marry a pagan princess was, sadly, not newsworthy. There were surely political reasons for this union. But there were no doubt other explanations too. Ahab, like every other ruler of the northern kingdom before and after him, was indifferent to the Word of the Lord and allowed pagan practices to influence him. Ahab reminds us that when a person is open to anything and everything, he or she ends up believing in nothing.

Ahab's new bride, Jezebel, on the other hand, was over-the-top religious. As a rabid evangelist for Baal, the pagan god of her people, she was violently opposed to the worship of Yahweh, the acknowledged God of her adopted nation.

Perhaps in an effort to insure "domestic tranquility," Ahab tried to accommodate the religious preferences of his strong, Baal-loving wife. He ordered his work crews in Samaria to build a temple for Baal worship. To be inclusive, he also had his men construct some sites for the worship of Asherah, a Canaanite goddess. That's when things got interesting.

God sent Elijah to Ahab with a short, not-so-sweet message: "As the Lord God of Israel lives . . . there will be no dew or rain during these years except by my command!" (1 Kgs 17:1). From the moment Elijah disappeared, the nation's water supply began to disappear as well. The drier things got over the ensuing months, the more enraged Jezebel and Ahab became. With murder in their eyes, they searched futilely for Elijah. When they couldn't find the prophet responsible for the drought that was destroying the nation, Jezebel began killing any prophet of Yahweh she could find (see 1 Kgs 18:4).

Three years passed before Elijah showed up again. This time he instructed Ahab to gather all the Israelites and all the prophets of Baal and Asherah (850 total) to Mount Carmel.

In the epic spiritual contest that followed, Elijah humiliated Jezebel's false prophets. Despite hours of elaborate actions performed by his prophets, Baal was silent, even absent; meanwhile Elijah's prayer resulted in a miraculous display of fire from heaven. "When all the people saw it, they fell facedown and said, 'Yahweh, He is God! Yahweh, He is God!'" (1 Kgs 18:39). Elijah commanded the people to seize the pagan prophets. When they did so, he slaughtered all 850 on the spot. When he gave the word for the rains to return, it wasn't long before everyone had to reach for their umbrellas.

Jezebel, for some unstated reason, was not present at this mountaintop meeting. When Ahab got home with the grim report, she blew a gasket, vowing to kill Elijah within twenty-four hours. Though her boast sent the weary prophet running like a scalded dog, it was a silly, arrogant threat. How did she think she was going to lay hands on the one who was in the hands of the one true God?

The drought, the events on Carmel, the rain—one would think this series of miraculous events would have been enough to pierce even Jezebel's heart. Sadly, she was unfazed.

Scripture records one final incident involving this wicked woman (see 1 Kings 21). Ahab coveted his neighbor's vineyard and offered to buy it, but the neighbor refused. So Jezebel concocted an elaborate scheme to accuse the neighbor of blasphemy and treason. In no time, she had him stoned to death and was in the process of seizing his land. The whole thing might have worked, but out of the blue came her old nemesis, Elijah. He pronounced doom on the house of Ahab and declared that Jezebel would eventually become dog food.

And so it happened—a fitting end for her deplorable, regrettable life (see 2 Kgs 9:30–37).

THE TAKEAWAY

Check yourself. Do you consistently demand that things go your way in your business dealings or personal interactions? Are people afraid of you? Do they walk on eggshells around you?

It's one thing to be a strong, capable, confident person who uses your abilities and position for good. It's another thing to be domineering and conniving and to exploit advantages for selfish ends.

Jezebel was in the second category. Her philosophy was "my way or the highway." She desperately needed to know and to embrace two Scriptural truths:

- "Pride comes before destruction, and an arrogant spirit before a fall" (Prov 16:18).

- "Don't be deceived: God is not mocked. For whatever a man sows he will also reap" (Gal 6:7).

Those are good truths for all of us to keep in mind all the time.

FOOD FOR THOUGHT

1. By marrying Jezebel, how did Ahab risk his own relationship with God and his nation's relationship with God?

2. When does healthy assertiveness cross the line into unhealthy, Jezebel-like behavior?

3. What counsel would you give to someone who has a spouse, boss, coworker, or neighbor who is demanding and calculating like Jezebel?

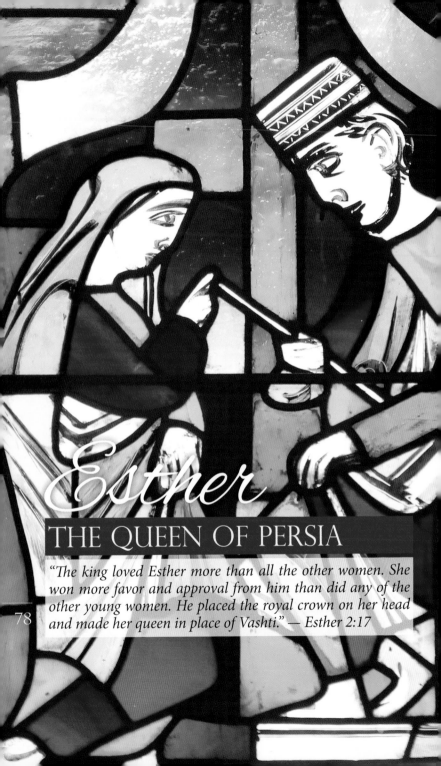

Esther

THE QUEEN OF PERSIA

"The king loved Esther more than all the other women. She won more favor and approval from him than did any of the other young women. He placed the royal crown on her head and made her queen in place of Vashti." — Esther 2:17

The book of Esther is curious. It's the only book in the Bible that never overtly mentions God. It contains no references to the Mosaic law or to sacrifices. You don't see priests making offerings here, or saints singing psalms, or prophets pointing the people back to God's promises.

Instead, Esther reads like the sort of novel people take on a beach vacation. It's full of harems, schemes, plot twists, intrigue, and suspense.

The story goes like this: Esther's Jewish name was actually Hadassah, but nobody much called her that, probably because she was born near the end of Old Testament history, during the period of the Babylonian exile. When Esther's parents died, she was adopted by her older cousin Mordecai. Later, when the Persians defeated the Babylonians, the victorious King Cyrus told all the Jews in Susa they could return at last to their homeland. Mordecai and Esther—along with many of their fellow Jews— chose to stay in Susa.

In Esther 2:7, we learn that Esther "had a beautiful figure and was extremely good-looking." Translation: she was beauty-pageant material. This was extremely fortunate, because it just so happened that Persia's new king, Ahasuerus (aka Xerxes), was having a national "beauty contest" to find a new queen. (He had recently dumped his old queen, Vashti, for embarrassing him in front of all his dignitary friends at a fancy feast.)

Gorgeous, young Esther was chosen to become part of the king's harem. When her turn came to spend the night with the king, she wowed Ahasuerus, who "loved Esther more than all the other women. She won more favor and approval from him than did any of the other young women. He placed the royal crown on her head and made her queen in place of Vashti" (Esth 2:17).

The plot thickens: Mordecai overheard some men planning to assassinate the king. He sent word to Esther, the plot was foiled, the assassins were hung, and the events were recorded in the royal record.

Enter Haman, the villain of this piece. An insufferable suck-up to the king, Haman had managed to secure a royal decree requiring people to bow whenever he was present. Mordecai stubbornly refused. This disrespect enraged Haman. When he learned of Mordecai's ethnic identity, Haman decided to kill Mordecai and all his people, the Jews, throughout the Persian kingdom (see Esth 3:6).

Clueless King Ahasuerus, oblivious to his queen's Jewish heritage, went along with Haman's plan. The date of the genocide was set and announced.

Devastated, Mordecai appealed to Esther "to approach the king, implore his favor, and plead with him personally for her people" (Esth 4:8). Esther, initially reluctant, reminded her cousin that Persian law explicitly stated that anyone initiating an audience with the king was subject to the death penalty.

Mordecai replied, "If you keep silent at this time, liberation and deliverance will come to the Jewish people from another place, but you and your father's house will be destroyed. Who knows, perhaps you have come to your royal position for such a time as this" (Esth 4:14). With great courage, Esther agreed to stick her neck out, saying, famously, "If I perish, I perish" (4:16).

She didn't perish. In fact, her story ends with a wonderful divine twist. While Esther planned a banquet in order to appeal for her fellow Jews—and while Haman was having gallows built so he could hang his nemesis, Mordecai—King Ahasuerus learned that Mordecai was the one who saved him from assassination!

In the end, the king made Haman honor Mordecai. Then, when Esther revealed her Jewish ancestry to his highness—and that Haman's plan would have meant her death—the king had Haman hanged on the very gallows he had built for Mordecai!

Because of Esther's beauty, bravery, and wisdom, the Jews were spared. They were able to defend themselves against their enemies. The Jewish holiday of Purim is still practiced today as a celebration of this victory (see Esth 9:16–32).

THE TAKEAWAY

The seemingly secular book of Esther reminds us that God is still God whether or not his creatures acknowledge him. Even in godless societies, even among secular people, God is always at work, accomplishing his plan for individuals and for the world. Unbelievers may speak of coincidence or luck, but the people of God see beneath the surface to a faithful and gracious heavenly Father who is always at work.

Perhaps the best personal lesson we can glean from Esther is her resolve in the face of danger to use her position and influence to try to help others, no matter what the personal cost.

FOOD FOR THOUGHT

1. Even though God is never mentioned in the book of Esther, how is his hand at work in the lives of his people evident throughout the story of Esther?

2. What do you think of Esther's involvement in the king's harem—and yet she's a Bible hero?

3. It's pure speculation, but why do you suppose Esther and Mordecai didn't return to their Jewish homeland when given the opportunity?

81

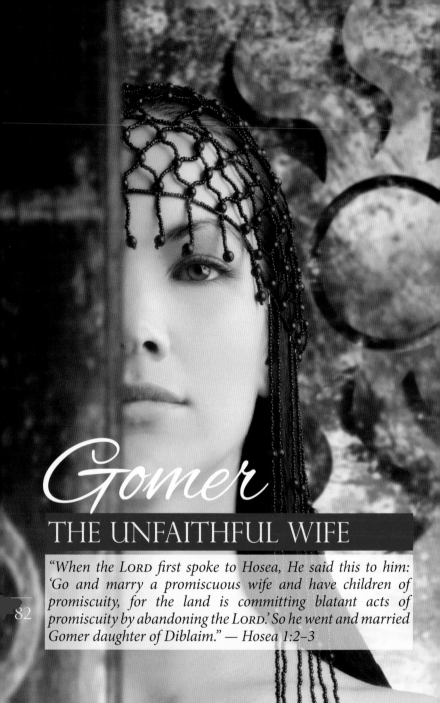

Gomer

THE UNFAITHFUL WIFE

"When the LORD first spoke to Hosea, He said this to him: 'Go and marry a promiscuous wife and have children of promiscuity, for the land is committing blatant acts of promiscuity by abandoning the LORD.' So he went and married Gomer daughter of Diblaim." — Hosea 1:2–3

The story of Gomer reflects the story of the northern kingdom of Israel and the southern kingdom of Judah in the eighth century BC. After being chosen by God, then faithfully loved and generously blessed by him for centuries, God's people got bored. Deciding they wanted a more exciting "religious life," they began to cheat. They turned to other gods.

This both angered and saddened God. He was very much a husband to the people of Israel (see Isa 54:5). The joint covenant they had made at Sinai was essentially a marriage agreement (see Exod 24:3–11). They had willingly, even gladly, pledged to be faithful. And now they were blatantly cheating on Yahweh. They shamelessly "moved in" with their other gods and made no attempt to hide their illicit dalliances.

God was furious and heartbroken all at once. He sent a prophet named Hosea to speak to his rebellious bride. In addition to asking Hosea to deliver a series of both tough and tender messages, God expected him to do something shocking and unthinkable: to give his people a vivid picture of their gross unfaithfulness, God actually commanded his prophet Hosea to marry a sexually immoral woman!

The woman's name was Gomer. We know almost nothing about her, except that she was the "daughter of Diblaim." (This fact alone is strong evidence that Gomer was a real person and not just a made-up character in a morality lesson.) We don't know if Gomer was already a known prostitute when Hosea popped the question or if she only became promiscuous *after* saying "I do." We just know this unlikely couple married.

And we know that whatever we decide to call Gomer—prostitute, unfaithful wife, adulterer—she ran around on Hosea. Morally untethered, she hopped in and out of strange men's beds. People gossiped with glee about "the prophet and the prostitute." They shook their heads and clucked their tongues in disgust. Can you imagine the embarrassment, the hurt, the disgrace for Hosea?

To complicate matters, Gomer gave birth to three children, the paternity in each instance being a subject of great debate. Her firstborn son was named after the famous Valley of Jezreel, prophesying a day of reckoning yet to come (see Hos 1:3–5). Next was the daughter Hosea named Lo-ruhamah, or "No Compassion" (1:6–7). Finally, a son was given the worst name of all, Lo-ammi, or "Not My People" (1:8–11).

And yet, even as Hosea kept coming up with disturbing names that broadcast bad news every time the kids were called to dinner, he also continued to care about his wayward wife. At her lowest point, Gomer ended up for sale in a disgraceful sort of slave market. In a remarkable act of grace, Hosea purchased her freedom and brought her back home. She isn't mentioned by name again in the Bible, though her shameful unfaithfulness is the vivid backdrop for all of Hosea's sermons.

THE TAKEAWAY

Before we get too outraged at Gomer's shocking immorality—and before we embrace a "holier than thou" attitude toward the ancient nation of Israel for its scandalous unfaithfulness to God—we would do well to look in the mirror. To be human, to be a son of Adam or a daughter of Eve, is to be spiritually promiscuous.

To be sure, we have our moments when we desire God, even love and serve him. It's not that we never give him our attention and affection and allegiance. The problem is we have a tendency to stray. Our eyes start roaming, and before we know it we are despising his faithful love and giving our fickle hearts to another. If the Great Commandment is to love God with every part of our being (see Mark 12:28–31), the Great Sin is to divert our love to someone or something else.

The hard-to-read, soap opera-ish story of Gomer and Hosea is in the Bible to remind us that when we sin, we don't just break some abstract moral code. We break the very heart of God. There's not a more gut-wrenching picture anywhere of God's anguish when his people turn away.

More importantly, Gomer's experience reminds us that God stays even when we stray. Paul would later say in the New Testament, "If we are faithless, He remains faithful, for He cannot deny Himself" (2 Tim 2:13).

The prophet Hosea, speaking for God, put it most poignantly: "My people are bent on turning from Me. Though they call to Him on high, He will not exalt them at all. How can I give you up, Ephraim? How can I surrender you, Israel? . . . I have had a change of heart; My compassion is stirred! I will not vent the full fury of My anger; I will not turn back to destroy Ephraim. For I am God and not man, the Holy One among you" (Hos 11:7–9).

FOOD FOR THOUGHT

1. What do you think about God using his prophet for a national object lesson?

2. What do you suppose it was like for Gomer to be rescued by the very husband she'd jilted?

3. What can we do practically and specifically to guard against spiritual unfaithfulness?

Mary

THE MOTHER (AND FIRST DISCIPLE) OF JESUS

"On the third day a wedding took place in Cana of Galilee. Jesus' mother was there, and Jesus and His disciples were invited to the wedding as well. When the wine ran out, Jesus' mother told Him, 'They don't have any wine.'

"'What has this concern of yours to do with Me, woman?' Jesus asked. 'My hour has not yet come.'

"'Do whatever He tells you,' His mother told the servants." — John 2:1–5

Mary had a front-row seat for an unbelievable life full of amazing stories: the angel Gabriel showing up out of the blue to tell her that she, a virgin, was *pregnant* (see Luke 1:26–38)—and not just expecting, but expecting *the Son of God*; the baby's birth in an animal shed far from home (see Luke 2:1–7); the odd parade of well-wishers saying beautiful and occasionally frightening things (see Matt 2:1–12; Luke 2:8–38); the mad dash to Egypt to escape Herod's wrath (see Matt 2:13–14).

After Herod's death, Mary and her husband, Joseph, eventually returned to the land of promise and settled again in Nazareth (see Matt 2:19–23). They had other children (see Matt 13:55). But her oldest son, the one the angel had insisted they name *Jesus* (which means "the Lord saves"), was different.

When he was twelve, she watched him dumbfound the religious experts at the temple in Jerusalem (see Luke 2:41–50). When he was a young adult, she had to watch him leave home in obedience to the call that was infinitely deeper than her own fierce love.

Every veteran mom knows that parenting is a whole lifetime of learning to let go. The mother of a son knows this truth even more acutely: *I can't keep him. He has to live his life.* For Mary it was deeper and more excruciating than even that: *I can't keep him. He has to give his life.*

She was there for his first miracle—providing exquisite wine for a wedding reception in Cana of Galilee (see John 2:1–11). She heard the stories of his skyrocketing popularity. Perhaps for a time she thought back to the old gentleman she'd met at the temple, just eight days after Jesus' birth (see Luke 2:25–35), who had spoken of ominous things, warning of opposition to this child so intense it would pierce Mary like a sword. As public sentiment grew for Jesus to become Israel's next king (see John 6:15), one wonders if Mary thought, *Maybe the old man at the temple was wrong—maybe he was just a kindly old fool.*

If she had such thoughts, she was jerked back to reality when she heard the reports of her son's increasingly heated verbal confrontations with the Pharisees and scribes. Then, when someone told her the Sadducees and Sanhedrin were getting involved, she felt nauseated. Vicious political enemies and bitter religious foes aligning in lockstep against her son? Her mother's intuition told her, *This is it; you need to be there.* So she went.

Mary was there when the Roman authorities (with the full approval of the Jewish leaders) took her oldest boy, hammered his battered and naked body to a wooden cross, and lifted him up before the mocking crowd.

Helpless to do anything, she could only shake with grief as she watched his precious life ebb away. She was there when he drew his final breath.

You have to believe she was never able to forget the gruesome images of those terrible hours. You hope that somehow they paled next to that beautiful gesture by Jesus in his final moments when, from his bloody perch, he arranged for his mom's care (see John 19:25–27).

The Bible isn't clear if Mary was there for all the joyous confusion surrounding Jesus' resurrection, but she is mentioned a few weeks later as being with the group of disciples who were waiting in Jerusalem for the outpouring of God's Spirit.

It's worth noting that the last recorded words we have of Mary are found in John 2:5: "Do whatever He tells you." And maybe at the end of it all, that's how she would most want to be remembered—less as Jesus' loving mother and more as his obedient follower.

TAKEAWAY

Some people incorrectly (and unhealthily) revere Mary. Others don't honor her near enough. She wasn't (and isn't) divine, but she is most definitely worth studying— and emulating.

When called as an unmarried virgin to become the mother of the Messiah (with all the difficult social implications that came with it), her response was immediate

and utterly submissive: "I am the Lord's slave . . . May it be done to me according to your word" (Luke 1:38).

We marvel at that kind of surrender, but Mary's reply sounds an awful lot like the attitude displayed by her son Jesus when he faced his own excruciating calling. He told his Father in heaven, "Not My will, but Yours, be done" (Luke 22:42).

We speak of kids being like their parents. In this case, it was the other way around.

FOOD FOR THOUGHT

1. Have you ever been chosen for something wonderful? Have you ever been approached about tackling a tough or unpleasant task? How was Mary's calling like both situations?

2. What characteristics about Mary are you drawn to?

3. If you could ask Mary any question, what would it be and why?

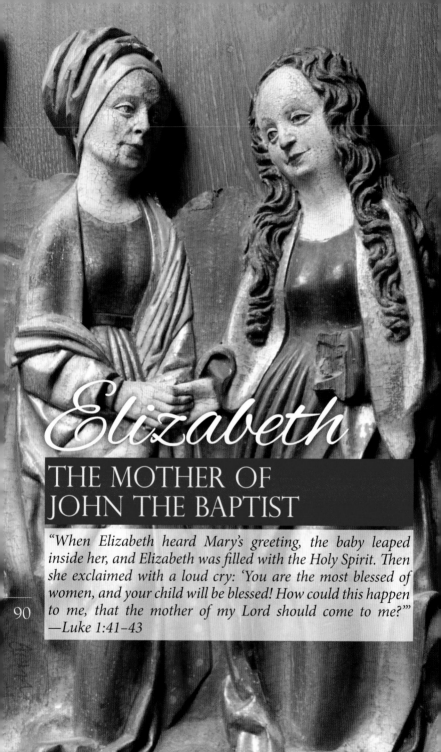

Elizabeth

THE MOTHER OF
JOHN THE BAPTIST

"When Elizabeth heard Mary's greeting, the baby leaped inside her, and Elizabeth was filled with the Holy Spirit. Then she exclaimed with a loud cry: 'You are the most blessed of women, and your child will be blessed! How could this happen to me, that the mother of my Lord should come to me?'"
—Luke 1:41–43

E lizabeth, mentioned only in Luke's Gospel, was married to a priest named Zechariah. "Both were righteous in God's sight, living without blame according to all the commands and requirements of the Lord" (Luke 1:6).

Yet in a culture where children were viewed as a primary evidence of God's blessing, they were also childless. Elizabeth was unable to conceive. This barrenness was a source of deep disgrace to her (see Luke 1:25). Only those who've suffered through fertility issues can fully appreciate the sting of all those unanswered prayers, the piercing pain of an empty nursery. Since Elizabeth and Zechariah "were well along in years" (Luke 1:7), it's not unreasonable to assume that they had given up the hope of ever becoming parents.

Then one day while Zechariah's priestly group ("Abijah's division," Luke 1:5) was on duty at the temple, he was chosen by lot for the special honor of burning incense in the holy sanctuary. As Zechariah performed this priestly duty, an angel of the Lord appeared to him. The angel informed him that God's answer to their many prayers for a child hadn't actually been no; it had been "not yet." But now, at last, it was time.

Elizabeth would have a son, the angel said. They were to name him John, and he would be a great man of God who would "turn many of the sons of Israel to the Lord their God" (Luke 1:16). He would, in fact, be the forerunner of the Messiah.

This was good news—great news, even. But to Zechariah, it was also a little far-fetched, given his and Elizabeth's advanced ages. They were more suited for a visit to the geriatric ward than the maternity ward. When Zechariah told the angel as much, he was (literally) struck speechless.

Nevertheless, the Lord kept his promise and opened Elizabeth's womb. When she discovered she was expecting, she did the first-century equivalent of taking a break from social media, social everything. She stayed home, watching her belly grow and marveling at God's grace.

Six months after appearing to Zechariah, the angel appeared to Mary to give out more exciting baby news: "Mary . . . You will conceive and give birth to a son, and you will call His name Jesus" (Luke 1:30–31).

When the angel explained that Mary's child would be "the Son of God" (Luke 1:35), Mary was dumbstruck, and perhaps tempted to doubt. So the angel added, "Consider your relative Elizabeth—even she has conceived a son in her old age, and this is the sixth month for her who was called childless. For nothing will be impossible with God" (Luke 1:36–37).

Mary packed her bags and hurried off to visit her relative. Whether this means Elizabeth was Mary's aunt or cousin or in-law, we're not sure. We just know that Elizabeth was beginning her third trimester when the freshly pregnant Mary arrived. The reunion scene that took place is both miraculous and heartwarming.

Two *"impossibly pregnant"* women (one elderly and one a virgin) and their two *unborn sons* (related by blood, connected by calling, and destined to make an eternal difference in the world) combined to make for *one great worship service!*

Elizabeth, finding herself filled with the Holy Spirit, erupted in gladness when she saw "the mother of [her] Lord" (Luke 1:43). She then reported that she had felt her baby leap for joy *in utero* when Mary called her name. Mary responded to this report by spontaneously bursting into song herself (see Luke 1:44–55).

Mary ended up staying with Elizabeth for almost three months. One can only imagine the many late-night conversations these two first-time expectant moms enjoyed over those weeks.

When Mary departed, it was time. Elizabeth delivered her son. As commanded, they named him John. And Zechariah's speech was restored. Filled with the Spirit, the proud new papa prophesied over this miracle child who would pave the way for his even more miraculous relative.

Elizabeth's late-life pregnancy is proof of the angel's statement that "nothing [is] impossible with God" (Luke 1:37).

THE TAKEAWAY

Elizabeth has something to say to every discouraged and despondent person: When you think your dreams are dead, think again. You don't have a clue to what our good and sovereign God is up to. At any given moment he is doing ten trillion things, and we are aware of maybe two or three of them. We surely can't see all the things he's orchestrating, all that might unfold tomorrow, what doors might open, what prayers are in the process of being answered. So keep praying and keep trusting. Don't give up. When you are least expectant, that's when you should probably get ready.

FOOD FOR THOUGHT

1. What do you wish you knew about Elizabeth that you don't know?

2. Why do you think Elizabeth went into seclusion when she found out she was pregnant?

3. What are the "impossible" things in your life right now? How can you become less cynical and more hopeful when thinking about those situations?

Anna

FAITHFUL TO THE VERY END

"*There was also a prophetess, Anna, a daughter of Phanuel, of the tribe of Asher. She was well along in years, having lived with her husband seven years after her marriage, and was a widow for 84 years. She did not leave the temple complex, serving God night and day with fasting and prayers. At that very moment, she came up and began to thank God and to speak about Him to all who were looking forward to the redemption of Jerusalem.*" — Luke 2:36–38

Someone once remarked that growing old isn't a battle but a massacre.

Sadly, in most cases this is all too true. If we live long enough, we are forced to grieve a long, painful series of losses. As we age, we say farewell—usually to our careers, often to our health, sometimes to our memories, always to the independent lives we once knew. And the older we get, the more often we will have to stand in funeral homes and cemeteries and say goodbye to beloved family members and dear friends.

From what we learn from the quick Bible cameo Anna makes in the Gospel of Luke, it's safe to confidently assume that the "daughter of Phanuel, of the tribe of Asher" faced her share of such goodbyes.

Like a true gentleman, Luke refused to give Anna's exact age, saying only that she was "well along in years." Like a great writer, however, Luke wanted us to grasp how remarkable this lady was. And so he added a couple of tidbits of revealing information: how, after seven years of marriage, Anna was widowed for eighty-four more years. Any third grader can do the math. Anna was a centenarian and then some.

Yet even though her marriage was cut short, she was alone for most of her life, and she was among the most senior of Israel's senior citizens, nothing in Luke's description gives the impression that Anna felt sorry for herself. She wasn't a grumbler, and she certainly didn't sit around killing time, waiting for the end. In just a few words, Luke painted the picture of an alert, active, God-focused woman.

Anna was a prophetess. This means she received revelations and messages directly from God. From Luke's description ("she did not leave the temple complex"), it's clear Anna embodied the ancient words of King David: "How happy is the one You choose and bring near to live in Your courts! We will be satisfied with the goodness of Your house, the holiness of Your temple" (Ps 65:4).

Though she must have lost some of her vitality over the years, Anna continued to serve God "night and day with fasting and prayers." Can't you see her if you close your eyes—this faithful, hunched-over fixture at the temple? This slow-moving, salt-of-the-earth prayer warrior? Every temple and every church—in every era—could use 1,000 women just like her.

On one particular day, Anna was doing what she did every day of her precious life: listening for the voice of God and using her own voice to plead with God. Suddenly she became aware of a commotion nearby. She couldn't be sure, but it looked like Simeon, one of her older cohorts, talking excitedly with a young couple. He seemed to be cradling a baby in his arms and beaming as he looked up toward heaven.

Perhaps it was because Anna couldn't hear what he was saying that she shuffled over to where he was. She arrived just in time to hear Simeon exclaim, "My eyes have seen Your salvation" (Luke 2:30). And then Anna saw it too: this child was *the* child. This was the promised One she'd been waiting and praying for all her life.

Luke mentioned that for a few moments Anna joined Simeon in his impromptu worship service, profusely thanking God. Then, this elderly, God-loving woman went into evangelist mode, speaking "about Him to all who were looking forward to the redemption of Jerusalem" (Luke 2:38).

How long Anna lived after this day is a mystery, but if you were a betting person, wouldn't you wager that whenever it was, she died with a smile on her face?

THE TAKEAWAY

Anna, whose name means "grace," aged gracefully. Given her sad history, she might have turned bitter. She might have become self-absorbed.

But she rejected a life of self-pity and embraced a life of service. She would faithfully steward her prophetic gift. She would expend her energy and use her breath to pray. Rather than giving up, she would keep showing up and looking up. All those days, all those decades, she waited, wondered, and watched.

Such faithfulness guarantees we'll be in the right place at the right time.

FOOD FOR THOUGHT

1. Be honest—would most modern-day religious people view Anna as a role model or a kook? Why or why not?

2. When you consider Anna's long, unusual life, what quality or experience stands out most to you?

3. What's your plan for aging gracefully and being faithful to the very end of life?

A Bleeding Woman

Woman

REACHING OUT FOR CHRIST

"'Daughter,' He said to her, 'your faith has made you well. Go in peace and be free from your affliction.'" — Mark 5:34

Three of the four Gospels tell her story (see Matt 9:20–22; Mark 5:25–34; Luke 8:43–48), yet we don't know her name. We don't even know the name of her medical condition, only that she had some sort of incurable bleeding disorder—possibly hemophilia or, more likely, something gynecological in nature.

If it were a chronic menstrual disorder, this poor woman was probably relieved to be anonymous. Such a condition would have made her, according to Jewish ceremonial law, continuously "unclean" (Lev 15:25–27). Her presence at any sort of social gathering would have been unacceptable. Perhaps a lepers' colony would have welcomed someone like her. Perhaps.

Hers was a grim, hopeless life: all the embarrassing personal and practical considerations; all the tricky social ramifications. If you've ever had an illness that the so-called experts couldn't diagnose, much less cure, or if you've been perpetually weak, taken advantage of, pitied yet shunned, you know how she felt. Our unnamed friend learned quickly to make herself scarce, even invisible. She consigned herself to eking out a lonely existence in the margins and shadows.

That is, until the day she heard Jesus was in town.

She was in the second *decade* of her mystery illness. She had lost track of all the doctors she'd consulted, all the money she'd spent on treatments that proved worthless. And now the traveling teacher with the reported power to heal the sick was just up the road.

Thinking, *What if all the stories I've heard are true?* or *What have I got to lose?,* she took off.

Jesus wasn't hard to find. She simply looked for the big, boisterous crowd. Then she listened to the excited chatter all about her. He was in the center of this mob, all right, heading to someone's home to attend to a sick child.

Figuring, *This is my chance*, she began to work her way through the jostling, joyful masses. A handful of people recognized her, gave her horrified looks, and quickly stepped aside (the one and only time her illness had ever benefited her).

In a matter of moments, she was directly behind him. People were greeting him, grabbing at him, and patting him on the back. All this, even as his followers tried to form a human shield around him and push back the crowd.

99

She felt nervous and embarrassed and desperate all at once. But she also felt, from somewhere, a strange surge of confidence—or was it faith? Quickening her step, she muttered under her breath, "If I can just touch His robes, I'll be made well!" (Mark 5:28).

Lunging forward while stretching out her hand, she managed to brush her fingers against the cloth of his garment. It took only an instant, but instantly she knew the truth in her head. More importantly, she felt it in her body. She was *well*.

Before she could turn and blend back into the watching masses, Jesus stopped dead in his tracks. "He turned around in the crowd and said, 'Who touched My robes?'" (Mark 5:30).

While Jesus scanned the tightly packed crowd about him, his disciples essentially replied, "Who *hasn't* touched your robes?"

It was at this point that the woman who had been *made* clean by Jesus decided to *come* clean. She stepped forward, bowed at Christ's feet, and told him everything. "'Daughter,' He said to her, 'your faith has made you well. Go in peace and be free from your affliction'" (Mark 5:34).

It's not hard to imagine Jesus smiling as he said this to her. It's not hard to imagine our unnamed friend smiling for a long, long time after that moment.

THE TAKEAWAY

There's a lot to like in this obscure woman. Even when she was suffering greatly, she refused to quit. Despite being victimized repeatedly by hapless and shady doctors peddling worthless "cures," she refused to play the victim.

Think of all the courageous steps she took. She risked public ridicule and rebuke in leaving her isolation. Sick of being sick and wanting to get well, she exercised great initiative in seeking out Jesus. Finding him, she had the faith to reach for him, believing that one simple touch would make her well. When she was found out, she told Jesus "the whole truth" about her life and her actions (Mark 5:33). Even as she was honest with him, she was vulnerable in front of all the others.

As a result of such action-oriented faith, this woman went home well, healed by Jesus, commended by him, and set free from a long-term affliction.

This side of heaven we may not know this woman's name—but we know what adjectives describe her: tough and tenacious, bold and believing, humble and whole.

FOOD FOR THOUGHT

1. What is the toughest thing about battling a chronic medical condition?

2. In most cases, Jesus healed the sick by touching them. Here a sick woman received healing by touching him. How much should we read into that?

3. If you could touch Jesus (or be touched by him) and be healed of something or set free from something (not necessarily a physical malady), what would it be and why?

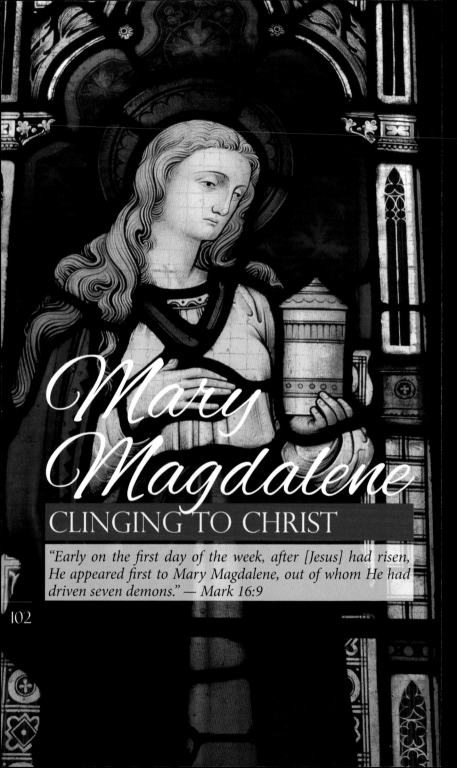

Mary Magdalene

CLINGING TO CHRIST

"Early on the first day of the week, after [Jesus] had risen, He appeared first to Mary Magdalene, out of whom He had driven seven demons." — Mark 16:9

When discussing the most devoted followers of Jesus, the New Testament writers say far less about three of the apostles—Bartholomew; James, son of Alphaeus; and Thaddaeus (likely the nickname for Judas, the son of James)—than they say about Mary Magdalene.

She was from Magdala, a small town in Galilee in northern Israel. And since *Mary* was such a popular name in the New Testament, people took to calling this particular Mary by her hometown.

At some point early in his Galilean ministry, Jesus encountered Mary Magdalene and cast seven demons out of her. Many have speculated that Mary was a former prostitute. In fact, movie renditions of the life of Christ through the years have often taken this creative liberty. We don't know if that's true. The Bible doesn't say. We don't know exactly how the seven evil spirits afflicted Mary. But from the grim descriptions of demon-possessed individuals elsewhere in the New Testament, it's safe to assume Mary endured a miserable existence.

That is, until Jesus came to where she was and set her free. Immediately, this transformed woman became one of Jesus' most committed disciples. She latched on to Christ like a drowning person grabs a life ring. You get the sense she didn't want to let him out of her sight.

She became part of his traveling entourage (along with a group of other devoted women; see Luke 8:1–3). They gave their time, energy, full attention, material resources—in short, their entire lives—to Jesus.

Over the course of Christ's three-year ministry, many of his followers or would-be disciples turned away (see Mark 10:17–23; John 6:66). Not Mary Magdalene. She clung to Christ like a person dangling over a cliff hangs on to a rope.

She was there at the foot of the cross on the awful day of his death (even when most of his male followers had gone into hiding; see Mark 15:40; John 19:25).

She was present at his hasty burial (see Mark 15:47) and returned to his tomb immediately following the Sabbath in order to properly anoint his body (see Mark 16:1).

Because of her devotion, Mary Magdalene—a woman with an awful past—enjoyed the privilege of being one of the first witnesses of the empty tomb on that first Easter morning (see Matt 28:1–7; Mark 16:1–7; Luke 24:1–8).

Still, it was too much to comprehend. In their shock and confusion, the women rushed to tell the apostles, who were skeptical and insisted upon seeing these things for themselves.

In the chaos and commotion of that mind-boggling morning, many of Christ's disciples, male and female, investigated the empty tomb. Eventually, however, they all left.

All except for Mary. (Are we really surprised?) This deeply grateful and devoted woman lingered. Clinging to her precious memories, she stood outside the tomb crying. Then she stooped to look inside. John tells us what happened next:

> She saw two angels in white sitting there, one at the head and one at the feet, where Jesus' body had been lying. They said to her, "Woman, why are you crying?"
>
> "Because they've taken away my Lord," she told them, "and I don't know where they've put Him." Having said this, she turned around and saw Jesus standing there, though she did not know it was Jesus.
>
> "Woman," Jesus said to her, "why are you crying? Who is it you are looking for?"
>
> Supposing He was the gardener, she replied, "Sir, if you've removed Him, tell me where you've put Him, and I will take Him away."
>
> Jesus said, "Mary."
>
> Turning around, she said to Him in Hebrew, *"Rabbouni!"*—which means "Teacher."
>
> "Don't cling to Me," Jesus told her, "for I have not yet ascended to the Father. But go to My brothers and tell them that I am ascending to My Father and your Father—to My God and your God." (John 20:12–17)

How fitting that in this happiest and most amazing of moments, Mary Magdalene instinctively did what she'd been doing ever since she met Jesus: she clung to him.

THE TAKEAWAY

There are those who scoff at faith in Christ, saying, *That stuff is for the weak. It's a crutch for spiritual and emotional cripples.*

It's not far-fetched to think that Mary, if she heard such comments, would only smile, nod, and say, "But of course! That's why I cling to him—and that's why everyone should."

Jesus would say, "The poor in spirit are blessed, for the kingdom of heaven is theirs" (Matt 5:3). And he would also say, "Those who are well don't need a doctor, but the sick do" (Matt 9:12).

FOOD FOR THOUGHT

1. What specific characteristics and qualities about Mary Magdalene make her someone who should be emulated for being a devoted follower of Christ?

2. In first-century Israel, women weren't allowed to testify in court; their testimony wasn't considered reliable. What does it say to you that the first witnesses of Jesus' resurrection were Mary Magdalene and other women?

3. Would other people look at your life and confidently say, "Now *there's* a person who clings desperately to Christ"? Why or why not?

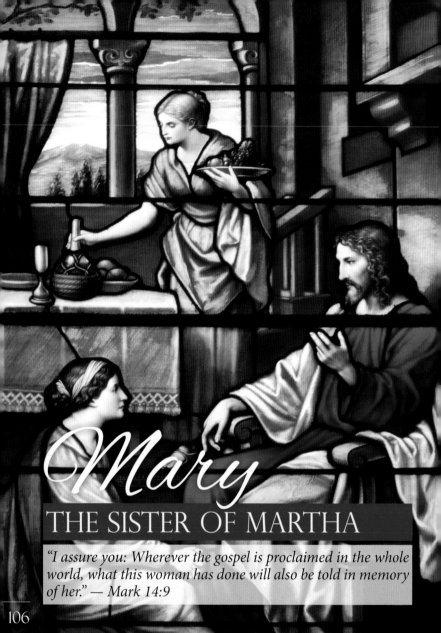

Mary

THE SISTER OF MARTHA

"I assure you: Wherever the gospel is proclaimed in the whole world, what this woman has done will also be told in memory of her." — Mark 14:9

The New Testament is full of "Marys." With six or seven different women sharing that same name, it's easy to get confused. The Mary we're looking at here was a resident of Bethany, near Jerusalem. She was the sister of Martha and Lazarus. We meet her in three separate stories in the New Testament.

In one, Mary seems to be *peeved at Jesus* (see John 11:20, 28–33). Her brother, Lazarus, had fallen deathly ill. She and Martha sent word for Jesus, a close friend, to come—and come *quickly*. Christ did not rush to help; in fact, he took so long that he missed the funeral. When he showed up four days after Lazarus's burial, Mary refused at first to go greet him.

In the other two incidents, Mary is *praised by Jesus*. There's the famous scene, mentioned only in Luke (10:38–42), where Jesus and his disciples showed up in Bethany right at dinnertime. While Martha frantically scrambled to get a meal on the table, Mary sat in the living room listening to Jesus. When Martha, in great frustration, insisted that Jesus tell Mary to lend a much-needed hand in the kitchen, Jesus gently chided her for being "worried and upset" about the wrong things. He then commended Mary for her proper priorities.

The other event in which Jesus affirms Mary is mentioned in three of the four Gospels (see Matt 26:6–13; Mark 14:3–9; and John 12:1–8. Note: despite similarities, this is different from the story found in Luke 7:37–50, which took place in Galilee). This encounter with Jesus happened near the end of Christ's life. Mary anointed him with some very expensive perfume during an elaborate feast thrown by Simon and Martha. Jesus' promise that Mary's actions in this moment would be forever "told in memory of her" (Mark 14:9) has been fulfilled a million times over. No doubt you've heard more sermons, done more Bible study lessons, and read more devotionals about this incident than you can remember.

But it's worth looking at again. Put yourself in Mary's place. Imagine yourself among the guests at this dinner party. Reclining at the dinner table is Lazarus—the brother you love so deeply and thought for sure you'd lost. You look over at Simon, the one who struggled for so long with the disfiguring disease of leprosy. The disciples are there, with all their amazing tales. Everyone in attendance has a story.

And there in the midst of them all is the guest of honor: Jesus of Nazareth, the carpenter-turned-rabbi. He's the One who brought your brother back from the grave. He's the One who made Simon well and whole. He's the One—you know it from firsthand experience—whose words are truth and life itself.

This is the *Savior*. The Messiah is in *your* house. Your heart is so full. You are beyond thankful. Then you remember it—your most precious possession. That alabaster jar of very expensive fragrant oil made from nard. It's a *big* jar, a pound or more, meaning it's worth a small fortune (at least a year's salary). It was to be part of your dowry one day. Whatever!

With excitement, you run to your room and retrieve it. Then with unbridled joy you bring it out and break it open. As the exotic fragrance fills the room, and as the partygoers gawk, you pour the precious substance on Christ's head. When it drips down on his feet, you kneel, undo your hair, and mop up the excess.

All conversation ceases. The room goes still. Eyebrows are rising. Eyes are cutting all about the room. Finally, Judas, one of the disciples, speaks. It's a critique, a negative statement about such "waste," followed by a disingenuous comment of how this fragrant oil could have been sold and the money donated to the poor. Other disciples join in the rebuke.

Jesus won't stand for it. "Leave her alone. Why are you bothering her? She has done a noble thing for Me. . . . She has done what she could; she has anointed My body in advance for burial" (Mark 14:6, 8).

An impulsive, appreciative gesture was made in a private dinner party a long time ago, and we're still talking about it today.

THE TAKEAWAY

If we had to guess, Mary wasn't trying to be noble when she anointed Christ. Nothing in any of the Gospel accounts suggests she was driven by thoughts like "I *should* do this" or "I probably *ought* to take this action." It was awe and gratitude, not a sense of duty, that propelled her to be so generous. Mary's actions remind us that no act of genuine love is ever wasted.

Are you a lavish person? When you feel grateful, are you generous with your words, your time, and your possessions?

FOOD FOR THOUGHT

1. What is it about human nature that gets critical when we see others living freely and generously?

2. Are you a grateful person? For what blessings are you most deeply thankful?

3. Of these two sisters, Mary seems more dreamy, impulsive, and expressive; Martha seems more action oriented, logical, and levelheaded. Which of the two personality types are you more like?

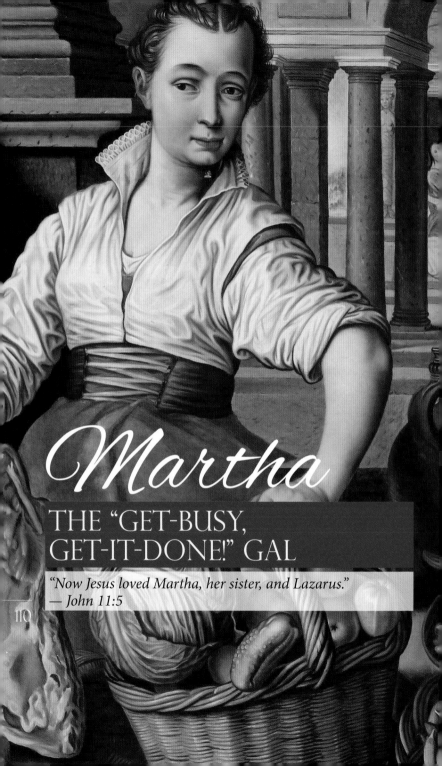

Martha

THE "GET-BUSY, GET-IT-DONE!" GAL

"Now Jesus loved Martha, her sister, and Lazarus."
— John 11:5

The New Testament informs us that Martha lived in the little village of Bethany (on the east side of the Mount of Olives, a couple of miles from Jerusalem). Some speculate she was married to the man known in the Gospels as Simon the Leper (compare Matt 26:6–7; Mark 14:3; and John 12:1–3).

What we know for sure is that Martha had a sister, Mary (see Luke 10:39), and a brother, Lazarus (see John 11:1–3).

From the limited glimpses the New Testament gives, we glean that Martha loved to entertain. She enjoyed having people in her home and doting on them. She was a worker bee, a high-energy, high-capacity force of nature who liked everything "just so."

You know the type. Driven by a strong vision of what needs to happen and armed with a long to-do list and a passion for excellence, they can turn the most mundane situation into a special, lavish occasion. Their motto? If a little pizzazz is good, more is better. Think hospitality, creativity, and efficiency all at once. If you can get a mental picture of all this, you are thinking of Martha.

Martha only shows up once in Luke's Gospel—in a funny little anecdote about an impromptu dinner party. It seems Jesus and his disciples were passing through Bethany (see Luke 10:38–42). Ever the "hostess with the mostest," Martha invited the whole gang over for dinner and then, like a domestic tornado, spun into action. Maybe she had no advance warning of their visit, or perhaps she was already edgy about other matters. Whatever the case, standing over her stove stirring all those boiling pots, Martha peeked out into the living room and saw a sight that made her blood boil. With a houseful of guests and a major meal to be cooked and served, Martha spied her oblivious sister, Mary, plopped on the floor listening to Jesus.

Exasperated, Martha marched over and scolded Jesus, "Lord, don't You care that my sister has left me to serve alone? So tell her to give me a hand" (Luke 10:40).

Jesus gently chided Martha right back. He more or less told her to relax, that an elaborate meal wasn't necessary, and that hospitality is about much more than fine china and gourmet fare.

John 11 gives us another glimpse of this endearing woman who loved by serving. We read there about Martha's brother, Lazarus, coming down with some sort of mystery illness. When his condition worsened, Martha and Mary sent for Jesus. When Jesus seemed to dawdle and delay, Lazarus died.

It wasn't until days later, after Lazarus had already been entombed, that the sisters got word that Jesus was on his way. Awash in grief and confusion, Mary holed up in her house. Not Martha. She made a beeline for Jesus. She intercepted him before he even made it to the city limits and blurted out:

> "Lord, if You had been here, my brother wouldn't have died. Yet even now I know that whatever You ask from God, God will give You."

> "Your brother will rise again," Jesus told her.

> Martha said, "I know that he will rise again in the resurrection at the last day."

> Jesus said to her, "I am the resurrection and the life. The one who believes in Me, even if he dies, will live. Everyone who lives and believes in Me will never die—ever. Do you believe this?"

> "Yes, Lord," she told Him, "I believe You are the Messiah, the Son of God, who comes into the world." (John 11:21–27)

You've got to love Martha. She's the tireless woman who fussed over Jesus and wanted him to feel special. She's the trusting woman whose first impulse was to look to Jesus to fix whatever was broken.

If you had to serve on a committee with her and pull off a big project together, Martha might be tough. But if you want an example of true faith and fervent service, you can't do better than this dear woman from the suburbs of Jerusalem.

THE TAKEAWAY

It's been said—wisely so—that every strength comes with a corresponding weakness. So, for example, the person who is extremely gentle and kind may have a tendency to avoid saying hard, but needed, words. Or the leader with the giant vision can ride roughshod over others in trying to reach a lofty goal if he or she isn't careful.

Martha was no exception to this fundamental rule of life. In her strong desire to honor Jesus, she got worked up and frustrated when Mary didn't get on board with her plan. Martha's good desire somehow morphed, and the result was an awkward experience.

Consider how you're wired. Think about how your weaknesses manifest themselves in certain life situations. If you're really brave, ask a trusted friend, "What would you say are my strengths and what would you say are my weaknesses?"

FOOD FOR THOUGHT

1. Read Luke 10:38–42. Is Jesus saying here that being active and servant minded like Martha is silly and unnecessary? Why or why not?

2. Why do opposites drive each other nuts (i.e., introverts vs. extroverts; people who are "all head" vs. people who are "all heart," etc.)? What's at stake if they can't get along? If they can?

3. Are you more like Martha or unlike her? Why?

113

Joanna

GRATEFUL AND GENEROUS

"Soon afterward He was traveling from one town and village to another, preaching and telling the good news of the kingdom of God. The Twelve were with Him, and also some women who had been healed of evil spirits and sicknesses: Mary, called Magdalene (seven demons had come out of her); Joanna the wife of Chuza, Herod's steward; Susanna; and many others who were supporting them from their possessions." — Luke 8:1-3

Joanna is mentioned by name only twice in the New Testament. Both occurrences are in the Gospel of Luke.

In Luke 8, we learn that Joanna was the wife of Chuza, a prominent man in the employ of none other than the notorious Herod Antipas. If that name doesn't ring a bell, he was one of the sons of King Herod the Great (the ruler who tried to murder Jesus shortly after his birth). Antipas inherited one-fourth of his father's "kingdom," thus his title "tetrarch" (Luke 3:1). During his life, Israel remained under the domination of Rome, meaning Herod Antipas's rule was limited in scope. Even so, he wielded great political power across the Galilean and Perean portions of the Holy Land.

To rise to the position of Herod's steward, Chuza had to have been extremely gifted and competent. Inherent in the title is the idea that Chuza enjoyed Herod's full trust. Typically, a steward functioned like a personal assistant/business manager/right-hand man. Stewards typically oversaw a wealthy person's property and holdings. In some cases, they even acted as a guardian or tutor of any children. Serving a top-ranking government leader in this capacity, Chuza would have enjoyed many perks. Chief among them would have been high compensation.

Because of Chuza's position, Joanna enjoyed more advantages, luxuries, and connections than most women. Imagine the first-century, Jewish equivalent of the modern, high-society, country-club set—this was Joanna's world.

But as we know, wealth and power are not enough to ward off the troubles of life. Those from the upper crust get sick. A-listers often see their lives come unglued. And so it was with Joanna. Either she suffered from some sort of serious medical malady or she (literally) battled demons in her soul.

We know this because Luke lists her among a group of women whose lives had been radically changed by Christ. Some of these had been healed physically. Others had been delivered from demonic oppression or even possession. Luke doesn't tell us into which category Joanna fell.

The only thing we know for sure is that she was beyond grateful. Interestingly, the name *Joanna* means "Yahweh is a gracious giver." Clearly, the day Jesus called Joanna by name and restored her was the day Joanna experienced the full implications of her name.

So thankful was she for the gift of total health (spiritual, physical, emotional) that she began dipping into her considerable financial assets to support his ministry efforts.

Did this cause tension at home or for her husband, Chuza, in his job? We don't know. Luke tells us that for an unspecified period of time, Joanna and several other women with experiences like her own became part of Christ's entourage. They traveled with Christ and the disciples "from one town and village to another" (Luke 8:1). Perhaps they shared their own personal testimonies of how Jesus had revolutionized their lives. Surely this caused eyebrows to rise and tongues to wag.

The only other mention of Joanna comes at the end of Luke's Gospel. She was one of the women who went to the tomb of Christ early on Sunday to anoint his body with spices. Upon arrival, they found the tomb open and the body gone. That's when they encountered "two men . . . in dazzling clothes" (Luke 24:4) who announced Christ's resurrection.

After this, Joanna fades from view. Where did she go? What did she do? No one knows. But it's safe to assume this grateful woman spent the rest of her days telling others of Yahweh's gracious gift of Christ and Christ's gracious gift of new life.

THE TAKEAWAY

One of the frequent charges leveled at Christianity is that it demeans women or at least denies them opportunities to use their strengths.

This surely wasn't Joanna's experience with Christ. After experiencing his gracious, healing touch, she became one of his most devoted followers. With obvious gratitude and enthusiasm, she generously shared her time,

energy, and resources. At great risk (perhaps marital, certainly social), she told others about her experiences with Christ. She was an influential force in the spreading of the gospel.

Married or not, a member of elite social circles or not, you too can have an impact for Christ and his kingdom. Look for occasions to share your story. Look for opportunities to meet needs.

FOOD FOR THOUGHT

1. If you could have lunch with Joanna, what questions would you want to ask her about her life and experiences?

2. In an era when a woman's testimony was regarded as inferior to a man's (if not invalid altogether), God revealed the resurrection of Jesus first to Joanna and her female friends. Why do you think God planned it that way?

3. *Joanna* means "Yahweh is a gracious giver." What are some of the gracious gifts God has blessed you with, and how could you better use or steward those for his eternal purposes?

The Samaritan Woman

MEETING THE THIRST QUENCHER

"Then the woman left her water jar, went into town, and told the men, 'Come, see a man who told me everything I ever did! Could this be the Messiah?' They left the town and made their way to Him." — John 4:28–30

I sn't it amazing how an entire life can change in a moment? That's the way it happened for the unnamed woman we meet in John 4.

On a nothing-special day in the Samaritan village of Sychar, she was minding her own business when she realized her household water jar was empty. It was unbearably hot out. *Perfect*, she thought. She probably wouldn't have to see anyone or talk to anybody. Grabbing her water jar, she slipped out the door.

Feeling like the neighbors were glaring at her through their windows, she quickened her step. Upon arriving at Jacob's Well, she froze. Slumped wearily against the stone was a young Jewish man. He was alone. When he asked her for a drink, she almost dropped her container.

Gathering herself, she managed to ask, "How is it that You, a Jew, ask for a drink from me, a Samaritan woman?" (John 4:9). The intriguing stranger sidestepped the question. Then he suggested that maybe, on second thought, he should be offering her "living water" (John 4:10).

A wise guy, she thought. "You don't even have a bucket," she observed (John 4:11). Before she knew it, she was in a deep conversation. He kept talking about thirst. And when he looked her into the eyes, it was like he was seeing straight into her heart. It was almost as if he was asking, "You're thirsty for a whole lot more than water, aren't you?" And of course, she was.

The clincher came when this kind but direct stranger gave her a matter-of-fact, accurate summary of her long and checkered marital past. Staring at the ground, she stammered uncomfortably, "I see that You are a prophet" (John 4:19). Part of her wanted to turn and run and save what little shreds of dignity she had left. Something else told her if she ran now, she'd never be saved. It was all so unexpected. She felt uncomfortable, unmasked, and unable to move.

She tried to reroute the conversation toward theoretical chitchat about obtuse religious matters. When that didn't exactly work, she tried to end the discussion by concluding, "I know that Messiah is coming. . . . When He comes, He will explain everything to us" (John 4:25).

That's when it happened—her life-changing moment. In response to her Messiah comment, the young Jewish man said simply, "I am He" (John 4:26). In other words, *I'm the One sent from God, the One you've been waiting for. And you're right. I can explain everything to you: how much the Father in heaven loves you and wants to have a relationship with you, why you feel so thirsty all the time, how you can finally satisfy the deep needs of your soul and break free from your addictive behaviors.*

Pierced to the heart by this unanticipated encounter, this unnamed woman set her water jar on the ground. Turning, she rushed lickety-split back to the village where everyone knew all her secrets.

Then the woman with the sordid past told about her spectacular encounter, and "many Samaritans from that town believed in Him because of what the woman said when she testified, 'He told me everything I ever did'" (John 4:39).

THE TAKEAWAY

Why was it such a big deal that Jesus would have a discussion at a local watering hole with a Samaritan woman? First, there was the gender gap. Middle Eastern customs said that an upstanding man must not engage in conversation in public with a woman who was not his wife. What Jesus did was shocking, even taboo.

Second, there was a huge racial and cultural barrier. Jesus was a Jew; this anonymous woman was a citizen of Samaria. The Samaritans were the product of the Assyrian invasion and subjugation of the northern kingdom of Israel in 722 BC. Intermarriage with foreign peoples who had been resettled in the promised land resulted in a race of people with mixed ancestry and diluted devotion to Yahweh. "Pure-blooded" Jews viewed Samaritans with contempt; the Samaritans responded with equal hostility. John's statement that "Jews do not associate with Samaritans" (John 4:9) was putting it mildly.

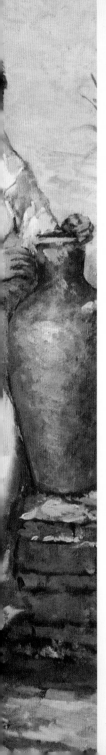

Third, there were issues of moral propriety. Jesus was a respected rabbi, a "holy man." This woman was regarded in her culture as a "sinner" and thus a social outcast.

In every way, Jesus' interaction with this woman was shocking. He crossed some huge barriers to engage her, to reveal eternal truth to her, and to call her to himself. This woman's encounter with Jesus reminds us of God's relentless love. It also screams the truth that life can change in a moment. Are you paying attention?

FOOD FOR THOUGHT

1. How can you apply how Jesus interacted with the Samaritan woman to the way you interact with other people?

2. How is physical thirst a good metaphor for the spiritual longings that we all have?

3. It seems like the Samaritan woman had been looking to male relationships to fill the void in her soul. What are some of the things you look to for security, a sense of well-being, significance, or meaning?

Phoebe
WOMAN OF IMPACT

"I commend to you our sister Phoebe, who is a servant of the church in Cenchreae." — Romans 16:1

The apostle Paul's letter to the Romans is widely regarded as his magnum opus. He began with eleven chapters that are *deeply theological*, essentially answering the question, "What does the gospel of Jesus really mean?" Then Paul wrote four more chapters that are *decidedly practical*, answering the question, "What differences does the gospel make in a believer's everyday life?"

Read the letter yourself and you'll quickly see why the great Martin Luther said, "This epistle . . . can never be read or pondered too much." By the time you get to the last word of Romans 15, you'll find yourself wanting to say "Amen" right along with Paul! And you'll be motivated to live for Christ.

Only, Romans 15 isn't the end of the book. The Spirit of God prompted Paul to tack on one more chapter. That chapter is *beautifully personal*. In Romans 16 Paul included thirty-five individuals by name! It's a tiny but fascinating window into the life of the early church. The first person we see there is a woman named Phoebe.

Paul didn't write much about her, and she's not found anywhere else in the Bible. But in two verses, Paul managed to paint a vivid picture of a competent and compassionate woman of tremendous impact. First, Paul wrote, "I commend to you our sister Phoebe." This introduction almost surely means this little-known woman was the courier who hand delivered Paul's letter to its recipients in Rome. Think of that. If Romans has ever touched your heart, you owe a small measure of gratitude to Phoebe. Before translators and Greek scholars and publishers ever got their hands on this sublime document, Phoebe carried it. What a privilege and what a responsibility to be the bearer of such news! Phoebe was commendable, in part because she was both available and reliable.

Second, Paul called her "a servant of the church in Cenchreae." The Greek word translated "servant" is the word *diaconos*, or in our vernacular, "deacon." Theology professors and ministers-in-training love to discuss and debate this verse and whether it describes (or even prescribes) an office of "deaconess" for the local church. Whatever view you take on that question, there's no debating the fact that Phoebe was a woman known for both her godly reputation and her tireless service in Cenchreae (a suburb of Corinth, Greece, where Paul wrote his letter to the Romans).

Finally, Paul urged the Roman Christians to "welcome her in the Lord in a manner worthy of the saints and assist her in whatever matter she may require your help. For indeed she has been a benefactor of many—and of me also" (Rom 16:2). Paul instructed the believers in Rome to show hospitality to this sister in the faith, this servant of the church. And why?

Because that's what saints (God's holy people) do. And also because Phoebe had been a "benefactor" to many, including Paul himself.

The word *benefactor* literally means "one who stands beside in order to hold up or assist." It was sometimes used in secular Greek writings to refer to a sports trainer, alert and at the ready to provide for the needs of his athlete. It broadly means "helper"; and more specifically in this context it means "supporter" or "patroness."

The strong indication is that Phoebe gave generously to the work of God. We don't know where she got her means or how she derived her income. But she apparently used her material resources to help fund the spread of the gospel. Add such financial generosity to the other ways she served and helped and supported the Lord's work. She spent her time tending to the spiritual needs of those in her Greek congregation as a "deaconess" (whether official or unofficial). She spent great effort traveling more than 600 miles from southern Greece to central Italy for the apostle Paul in order to deliver his world-changing letter. (Don't forget this was in an era when travel was far more dangerous and much less convenient.)

In just a few words—*sister, servant, benefactor*—Paul paints the picture of a caring, capable, courageous woman. Who wouldn't want to be described in those terms?

THE TAKEAWAY

Paul's quick glimpse into Phoebe's life and character is inspiring.

How did she become such a respected individual, praised and trusted by even the great apostle Paul? Phoebe's commendable life was built just like anyone else's—by one faithful act of service, one generous gift, one kind gesture at a time. Do that long enough and you'll have a great reputation. More importantly, you'll have an eternal impact. Most importantly, you'll honor God.

Phoebe was a true gospel girl. She loved God and loved people by giving her life away.

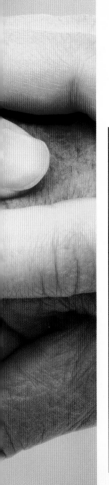

FOOD FOR THOUGHT

1. If you could eat lunch with Phoebe, what would you want to ask her?

2. From the information you know about Phoebe, what's most impressive to you about her life?

3. Some people (maybe Phoebe?) have an actual spiritual gift of serving or giving (see Rom 12:7–8); even so, all Christians are called to serve (see Gal 5:13) and be generous (see 2 Cor 9:6–7). Which is the bigger struggle for you: giving of your time and effort or giving your resources?

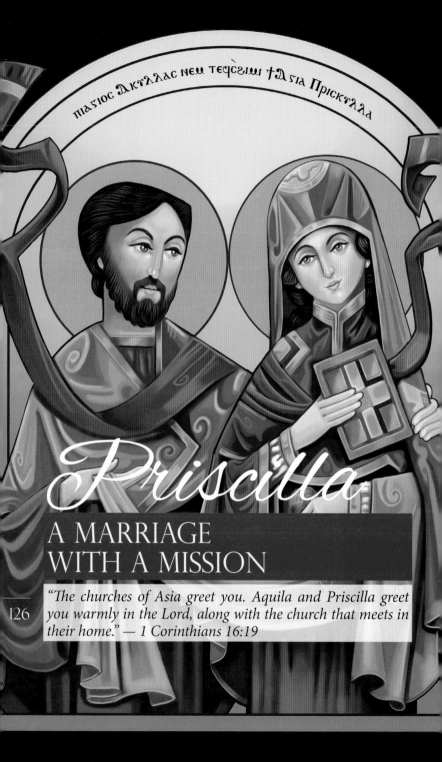

Priscilla

A MARRIAGE WITH A MISSION

"The churches of Asia greet you. Aquila and Priscilla greet you warmly in the Lord, along with the church that meets in their home." — 1 Corinthians 16:19

I t's impossible to think of Priscilla apart from her husband, Aquila. In six New Testament mentions, they are always named together. And while we don't have a lot of information about them, some "forensic Bible study" uncovers one of the more fascinating and inspiring couples in Scripture.

Luke, the writer of Acts, tells us this husband-wife team was originally from Pontus (the northern part of Asia Minor, modern-day Turkey). We know they lived and worked in Italy up until the time Claudius (the emperor between Caligula and Nero) expelled all Jews from Rome (see Acts 18:2). Then, relocating to Greece around AD 51, their lives changed dramatically: in Corinth they crossed paths with the apostle Paul.

Like Paul, Priscilla and Aquila were Jewish (see Acts 18:2). Like Paul, they were fervently devoted to the gospel of Christ (see Rom 16:3). Like Paul, "they were tentmakers by trade" (Acts 18:3). Not surprisingly, a deep friendship formed. We don't know if Priscilla and Aquila were childless or empty nesters. We only know that for an unspecified time in Corinth, Paul lived with and worked alongside this couple. Soon he began to minister with them.

When Paul sensed God's prompting to return to his sending church in Antioch, he set sail from Corinth—accompanied by Priscilla and Aquila. When their Syria-bound ship stopped briefly in Ephesus, Priscilla and Aquila agreed to stay behind in order to help minister to the fledgling church there (see Acts 18:18–21).

Aquila and Priscilla's impact in Ephesus was significant. Luke wrote about the arrival of a brilliant Jewish scholar named Apollos, a powerful communicator with an obvious love for Christ. However, when Priscilla and Aquila heard him teach in the synagogue at Ephesus, they realized his understanding of the gospel needed some fine-tuning. So they "took him home and explained the way of God to him more accurately" (Acts 18:26). Largely because of their hospitality and wise input, Apollos became an effective leader in the early church (see Acts 18:27–28).

For Priscilla and Aquila, such gospel-centered hospitality wasn't a one-time event. Three or four years later (AD 55 or early 56), Paul returned to Ephesus. Corresponding from there with the believers in Corinth, he wrote, "The churches of Asia greet you. Aquila and Priscilla greet you warmly in the Lord, along with the church that meets in their home" (1 Cor 16:19). Aquila and Priscilla weren't clergy—they ran a small business! But the picture that emerges is one of a gracious couple that warmly welcomed people into their hearts and home so they could love on them with the love of Christ.

A year or so later, Paul was in Corinth, writing from there a letter to the church at Rome. Notice what he said: "Give my greetings to Prisca [the more intimate form of Priscilla] and Aquila, my coworkers in Christ Jesus, who risked their own necks for my life. Not only do I thank them, but so do all the Gentile churches. Greet also the church that meets in their home" (Rom 16:3–5).

Amazingly, this well-traveled couple was back in Rome, picking up where they had left off years before. Another move, more ministry, greater impact. And *still* they weren't done. Some ten years later, Paul wrote his last letter. It was a reminder-filled note to Timothy (who was pastoring in Ephesus). In closing, the old apostle wrote, "Greet Prisca and Aquila" (2 Tim 4:19).

It's not hard to imagine a scenario in which Paul surely asked a final favor of his aging, long-term ministry partners: "Aquila and Priscilla, would you be willing to relocate one more time? My young protégé, Timothy, could sure use a couple with your wisdom and insight as he pastors in Ephesus."

It's not hard to envision them packing their bags that very day.

THE TAKEAWAY

If marriage is the union of two hearts and the merging of two lives, Aquila and Priscilla had a model marriage. What a great tandem for the gospel!

It's important to note that nothing in the New Testament suggests these two were highly educated, extremely wealthy, or phenomenally gifted. Mostly what they were was available and hospitable. They went wherever needed.

They opened their lives. They poured into other people. No doubt this was challenging and inconvenient. Surely it involved countless late nights and early mornings, oceans of coffee, mountains of meals.

But wherever they were, Priscilla and Aquila resolved to engage in the mission of God. They used their home as a powerful ministry tool. As a result, they had tremendous influence on at least three of the early church's most significant leaders—Paul, Apollos, and Timothy.

It's easy to make a mess in marriage. It's common to just make do. Priscilla (along with her husband, Aquila) encourages us to make something else—an eternal difference.

FOOD FOR THOUGHT

1. Married or not, how could you use your heart and home to welcome others in, to love people, to have an eternal impact?

2. What are the obstacles that keep you from embracing a ministry mind-set like Priscilla and Aquila had?

3. Who are the people who poured into you? Why not contact them and thank them today?

TOPICAL INDEX

SCRIPTURE INDEX

ART CREDITS

NOTES

NOTES